5·15

A Student's Guide
to Racine

KT-388-929

93

WITHDRAWN

A Student's Guide to Racine

by

PHILIP BUTLER

Professor of French
University of Wisconsin

HEINEMANN EDUCATIONAL BOOKS

LONDON

Heinemann Educational Books Ltd
22 Bedford Square, London WC1B 3HH
LONDON EDINBURGH MELBOURNE AUCKLAND
HONG KONG SINGAPORE KUALA LUMPUR NEW DELHI
IBADAN NAIROBI JOHANNESBURG KINGSTON
EXETER (NH) PORT OF SPAIN

ISBN 0 435 37582 2

Printed in Great Britain by
Spottiswoode Ballantyne Ltd.
Colchester and London

Contents

Foreword

This book is written mainly, as its title indicates, for under-graduates, although it is hoped it might attract sixth-formers and high school students who have developed an interest in Racine. The time is past of course when Racine was considered a good introduction to French literature – his simplicity! his clarity! so much more suitable for young minds than Rabelais or even Voltaire: *un auteur de tout repos*, who needed no bowdlerization. It so happened that some of the most important criticism of the last fifteen or twenty years has been centred on Racine. Using new approaches and modern methods, critics have reached views of Racine that are very far from the traditional ones, more complex, more difficult, more disturbing. They have in fact reached results that are sometimes sharply different from each other, or even incompatible.

I have tried at least to indicate some of those new directions, and, I hope, to induce readers to widen and deepen their knowledge of Racine. More generally speaking I have made full use of the rich literature of the subject, American and British as well as French, and Racinians will have no difficulty in ascertaining my debts, even though a book of this kind did not lend itself to a full apparatus of notes and references.

A Note *On Reading Racine* will be found at the end of the book. Those readers who are familiar with Racine can ignore it. Those who are not might start there.

P.B.

1

Racine and His Critics

For an author who has often been held up as a model of clarity and simplicity, Racine has gone in the last three centuries through a bewildering succession of opposite, often irreconcilable interpretations. He has been loved and hated in turn, praised beyond all reason, scorned beyond all justice, and he still retains after so much critical turmoil his enigmatic transparency. This alone, perhaps, should arouse at least some curiosity, and although this is no place for a detailed history of Racine's fame, a brief outline of the widely different reactions he has aroused may help new readers to a personal approach free from awed reverence or facile prejudice.

Racine in the seventeenth century

In his own time Racine had to run the gauntlet of comparison with the *grand Corneille*. What people did not find in his plays was the 'hero' who is, like Augustus, '*maître de lui comme de l'univers*'. What they did find in him, after Racine had eclipsed Corneille, was pathos, emotion, tears, an apparent simplicity far removed from the tense, complicated plots of Corneille, a subtle music that held them under its spell without their quite realizing its novelty. As for the theorists and *doctes*, who judged according to an elaborate system of rules, which they derived from Aristotle and his Italian commentators, they were not at first satisfied with Racine, but they were soon forgotten after the success of Boileau's *Art Poétique* in the 1670s. Tragedy in the *Art Poétique* was described after the Racinian rather than the Cornelian model, and ever since critics have marvelled at the regularity of Racine's plays and praised their conformity to classical rules. But it was Racine, not Boileau or the *doctes*, who created Racinian tragedy.

The eighteenth century

The long struggle between Racine's and Corneille's supporters did not end with the death of both playwrights, and it is still, in fact, going on. The eighteenth century, however, saw what may be called Racine's apotheosis, which was closely connected with a general view of the history of literature that prevailed at the time and for more than two centuries. At the time of the Renaissance, humanists like Rabelais and others had seen the medieval centuries as an age of darkness and barbarism; French critics, already in the seventeenth century and even more in the eighteenth, took over that scheme but in an altered form. When Louis XIV personally assumed the government of France (1661), the country was tired of half a century of internal strife and civil war. Louis ruled as an absolute monarch, but gave France law and order, and the peace she longed for. He also gave her unprecedented power in Europe, and the beginning of the 'personal reign' coincided with an extraordinary blossoming of talents: Corneille's last plays, most of the production of Molière, Racine, La Fontaine, Boileau, La Rochefoucauld, Retz, Mme de La Fayette, Lulli's operas, Le Vau's Versailles, can all be crowded into the twenty years that elapsed between 1660 and 1680. The contemporaries were genuinely dazzled by such multiple achievements, which the *Grand Roi* had, they thought, made possible, and when this time of greatness had gone, it appeared even greater in retrospect. Louis' reign – it lasted 72 years! – was identified with the seventeenth century which became for the French *le grand siècle*, or, as Voltaire put it, *le siècle de Louis XIV*. Not only the Middle Ages, but the sixteenth century were dismissed as Gothic, and the *siècle de Louis le Grand*, in which France had been greatest in literature, in arts, and in arms, became the century in which *l'esprit français* – as elusive a notion as the British national character, or the American way of life – had most fully realized itself. It took its place by the side of the *siècle de Périclès* and the *siècle d'Auguste*, but there was no doubt in France about which one was greatest. Its highest achievement lay in Racine's theatre, an unsurpassed model of tragedy, poetry, and style, which had reached perfection by its conformity to the eternal rules of reason and nature. The supreme realization of the French spirit was also the greatest expression of the human spirit: in *Athalie* Voltaire greeted '*le chef-d'œuvre de l'esprit humain*'.

It can be seen that there was a good deal of national conceit in such a conception, but it was a tight, coherent system, and it was accepted as self-obvious by generations of Frenchmen. Its first consequence was to impede the free development of any form of serious drama in France: immobilized, as in a strait-jacket, in the imitation of an inimitable model, French tragedy withered. Another result was to close French minds to the outside world. The discovery of Shakespeare could have been the opening of new vistas; it became the challenge of an outlandish barbarian to be stubbornly resisted, for what was at stake was the whole fabric of culture as conceived in France, the very existence of the 'classical scheme'. Whatever we may think of it, however, it would be highly unfair to make Racine responsible for this peculiar brand of cultural chauvinism, and in fact, if Racine was idolized, he was not always understood. What appeared admirable in him was *tendresse* rather than passion, the elegance of his style rather than the music of his verse, and the distinction and *noblesse* of his characters rather than the creation of a tragic universe.

The nineteenth century

It was not so much against Racine as against this universally accepted image of Racine that protest arose. In Germany Racine's tragedy was impatiently dismissed as mere courtly tragedy, *höfliches Drama*, a drama too cramped by etiquette and convention to allow the full expression of human passion. Schiller and Goethe turned to Shakespeare away from French imitation. In France the reaction of the 1820s took explosive proportions. In his somewhat flippant *Racine et Shakespeare*, Stendhal opposing Romantic and Classical literature defined the first as: '*l'art de présenter aux peuples des œuvres littéraires qui . . . sont susceptibles de leur donner le plus de plaisir possible*', and the second as '*la littérature qui donnait le plus grand plaisir possible à leurs arrière-grands-pères*'. Racine, according to Stendhal, had been a Romantic in 1670; in 1820 he was a Classic, and of no concern to us after the passing away of Versailles and the *Grand Roi*. Such a narrow historical view was still held by Hippolyte Taine in his *Nouveaux Essais de Critique et d'histoire* (1865). In Racine's tragedy Taine looked for nothing but French courtiers of the seventeenth century, and consequently found nothing else. His Racine is a great writer of no interest except as an historical document. From such a versatile, marvellously penetrating critic as Sainte-Beuve one could expect better. But Sainte-Beuve, who could resurrect forgotten authors and forgotten periods, was, when it came to challenging established ideas, surprisingly timorous. He had little to say about Racine that was new. By then anyhow the Romantic revolt had run its course. In a century seething with revolution, at the time of the shocking literature of Baudelaire and Flaubert, the now conservative bourgeoisie looked with nostalgia at the stability and conformism it earnestly wished to find in the writers of the seventeenth century. In a century of nationalisms the myth of the *grand siècle* was back in favour, and Racine was again ensconced as a national glory. For no better reasons foreign criticism was hostile to Racine out of Francophobia. English Victorian critics sadly distinguished themselves in that respect, and some of their more ridiculous pronouncements make one wonder if they had ever read the plays they dismissed with such withering contempt. 'The genius of Shakespeare is dramatic, that of Scott narrative and descriptive, that of Racine is didactic . . . he gives us . . . the commonplaces of the human heart . . . he enlarges on a set of obvious sentiments with considerable elegance of language and copiousness of declamation . . . Instead of laying bare the heart . . . of the sufferer . . . he reads us a lecture . . . but tragedy is human nature tried in the crucible of affliction, not exhibited in the vague theorems of speculation.' Why then was he so highly praised? 'Because nothing that is French can be barbarous in the eyes of this frivolous and pedantic nation'. Thus did Hazlitt pontificate in the *Plain-Speaker* – which did not trouble French critics at all: they retorted that Racine, or La Fontaine, or generally speaking the *chefs-d'œuvre de l'esprit humain* could not be understood by foreigners.

The twentieth century

The nineteenth century seems to have been an unhappy period for Racine, extolled or reviled for the wrong reasons. The twentieth began with two parallel attempts at rescuing him from the purely historical approach of the Romantics. G. Lanson tried to read into his plays what we might call a *drame réaliste*: Andromaque was the fearful mother, and Phèdre the *marâtre*; they were types that belonged to our time and to all times; their story could happen in all social classes and appear in the news any day in the columns of the *faits-divers*. A few years later Masson-Forestier created a kind of scandal by throwing a lurid light upon the hidden violence of Racine's drama, in which blackmail and perjury, incest and murder were common occurrences. These were the first attempts at a positive revaluation of Racine's art, and as such welcome. Both, however, were unsatisfactory. The *faits-divers* approach left out not only the poetic but the tragic element of the plays; tragedy is not a realistic drama. The Masson-Forestier thesis had the advantages and inconveniences of all theses: it set off aspects of Racine that had been overlooked or played down, but it ignored or devalued all others. The thesis itself was drowned in biographical pseudo-criticism and fashionable theories on race. From his cruel heroes Masson-Forestier assumed a tigerish Racine to whom his maternal ancestors, the Sconins, with their Scandinavian name, had brought the Viking blood which, apparently, explained Pyrrhus and Néron . . .

Racine could not, however, be fully understood and appreciated as long as he remained embedded, so to speak, in the so-called classical scheme of the *grand siècle*. The dismantling of this age-old construction was achieved in two movements, the first one mainly in France, the second mainly abroad. Perhaps the keystone of the old scheme was the notion of the *Ecole classique*. If *l'esprit français* had found its full realization in the *grand siècle*, it was through the intermediary of Boileau, who had apprehended it in its essence, and it was under the leadership of Boileau that Racine, Molière, La Fontaine had come together as a group. It was through listening to Boileau's voice and submitting to his advice that they had finally achieved perfection. Under the rigorous scrutiny of twentieth-century erudition the whole concept crumbled into nothingness; Boileau did not teach Molière how to write comedies, or Racine tragedies; the *Ecole classique* never existed.

Classicism and Baroque

The other aspect of the myth, that of a *siècle de Louis XIV* emerging with Malherbe and Corneille from a long night of Gothic barbarism, took longer to disappear. Sainte-Beuve already – as usual with much fearful provisos – had put back the sixteenth century on the map of French culture. As time passed on, the idea of medieval culture as the product of babbling childishness appeared increasingly childish. Finally the idea of the seventeenth century itself was also transformed. A century before, Victor Cousin had already insisted that if there was a *siècle de Louis XIV*, there was also, before 1650, a *siècle de Louis XIII*. And, in fact, the poetry of Théophile, Scarron, Saint-Amant, the dramas of Tristan and Rotrou, the comedies of the young Corneille aim at, and achieve, effects that are very far from those of La Fontaine, Molière, or Racine, but they are not to be shrugged off. They were born from a different society and a different civilization, and they are more akin to the Baroque culture that prevailed then all over Europe. The seventeenth century was not as homogeneous as was believed. and Racine's tragedies as well as Molière's comedies were not just the final step in a continuous development. They were in many ways a reaction against, a rejection of, a recent past, which the new poets shook off impatiently. They were not the docile application of ideal, pre-existent rules revealed through the illumination of Boileau, but strikingly original creations. Molière's world is sharply opposed to that of Corneille; La Fontaine's art is far more subtle than that of Malherbe; Racine's tragedies may, at first sight, resemble those of Corneille or Quinault, but below such superficial resemblances the differences are deep and many. Racine's heroes are of a different type; they live in a different world, according to values that are widely different from those of the Baroque age.

La Nouvelle Critique

It is, perhaps, only in the last fifteen or twenty years that the full consequences of the liberation of Racinian criticism have become evident. Just as the polemics around Racine had been a crucial element of the Romantic revolution, the more recent revolution of the *Nouvelle critique* has been centred on Racine. And it is not surprising that, after the collapse of the old historical–aesthetic interpretation of the classical scheme, attempts should have been made to integrate Racine's theatre into a new scheme based on up-to-date historical research, on modern, particularly Marxian, sociological concepts, or on a new, basically Freudian, psychology. L. Goldmann's important work on *The Hidden God* gives considerable emphasis to Jansenism as a socio-religious movement. Jansenism was a theological and moral system evolved by Cornelius Jansen, Bishop of Ypres, and his friend, Duvergier de Hauranne, Abbé of Saint-Cyran. Its conception of man's relationship to God was a particularly harsh one, and according to its enemies, the Jesuits, its conception of Grace, although based on Saint Augustine and Saint Thomas, was perilously near to Calvinistic predestination. The Jansenists, while vigorously refusing to be called Calvinists, were contemptuous of what they called the lax morality, the *morale relâchée* of the Jesuits, whom they accused of overindulgence towards the vices, prejudices, and customs of the society they lived in. L. Goldmann's book has three main parts. The first one throws new light on the origins and nature of Jan-

senism; the second examines the nature of the tragic vision in
Pascal; the third deals with Racine. For according to Goldmann, there are affinities and more than affinities between
Pascal and Racine, a common religious vision of man's condition, which has its roots in the particular social experience of
the particular social class from which they both sprang. It was
among those officers of the Crown belonging to the wealthy
bourgeoisie, the *noblesse de robe*, that Jansenist ideology found
a ready audience. And if it appealed to them it was because, as
a class, they found themselves in a particularly difficult predica-
ment: they depended for their very existence on the Monarchy,
while the Monarch was trying to limit and lessen their importance.

That Goldmann's research has considerably enlarged and
enriched our knowledge of Jansenism is not in doubt. That the
spread of Jansenism – among the high aristocracy as well as the
bourgeoisie – should be due to the not so tragic difficulties of
one limited portion of the *noblesse de robe* seems an unsatisfactory explanation. As regards Racine, the central importance
given by Goldmann to the tragic element is a very positive
factor, but is its origin to be found in the social experience of a
class of which Racine was never an active member? Misgivings
are not allayed when we come to the actual interpretation of the
plays. Too often it is dominated by the need to make them conform to the general thesis even at the cost of dismissing as
irrelevances or failures large slices of Racine's production: in
Britannicus Junie is the only character that may be called
tragic; in *Phèdre*, Phèdre is the only one who possesses reality,
and Hippolyte, Thésée, Aricie, Œnone simply have no existence; according to Goldmann they are puppets, *des pantins*,
just as Néron and Agrippine are wild beasts, *des fauves*, neither
of the two categories possessing any true value, and therefore
any real existence . . .

Ch. Mauron's *Psychocritique*

To some extent literature always is a social phenomenon, an
aspect of communication. But to what extent, and of what

nature is the link, that is the problem, and it may well be that Goldmann has over-simplified the complexity of Racine's social background: a much wider view must be taken into account of the new society that came into being after the *Fronde* in the second half of the seventeenth century. It can also be said, of course, that the social background is not everything, and that the personal response to the poet's surroundings is governed by personal elements which are often rooted in his early formative years. This is where Ch. Mauron's *Psychocritique* comes in. *L'Inconscient dans l'œuvre et la vie de Racine* (1957) is an attempt at making use of Freud's psychoanalytic findings to throw new light on the personality of Racine as a man and as a poet. This required a considerable work of adaptation. Psychoanalysis is meant to be a help to psychiatry in elucidating complexes which, because they are not consciously apprehended, create disturbances in the psyche. The obvious peril is to treat Racine like a patient whose neuroses have to be discovered to be cured. Apart from the fact that Racine has been dead for three centuries and is not in need of a cure, it is his plays that interest us, not his neuroses, if he had any. But of that peril Mauron is well aware, and if we object that his method can give only a partial view of Racine, he will answer that he does not expect more from it. Psychocriticism with him is a branch of literary criticism, not of psychiatry, and what it hopes to show is that Racine creates heroes, and puts them into situations which, in spite of their differences, have common, recurrent elements, because they go back to obsessions or *hantises* of Racine himself, who endlessly arranges or rearranges elements borrowed from history, legend, or myth, according to a pattern that remains fundamentally the same.

To follow Mauron, we must first recall a few facts concerning Racine's early life. He was a little more than one year old when his mother died. His father remarried, and gave him a new home, but died before the child was three. He was then taken care of by his grandparents, but after the death of his grandfather, his grandmother joined his aunt, who was a nun at the convent of Port-Royal; the sense of loss and insecurity of the infant, and also perhaps the early experience of death, marked him from the start. Later the death of his other grand-father, with whom he had no close relationship, seems to have affected him almost unreasonably. Fatherless heroes, children or youngsters, appear in several of his plays. Astyanax is the son of the dead Hector; Britannicus, of the murdered Emperor Claudius; Eriphile is the abandoned child who has never known her father or her mother; Eliacin's parents were massacred by Athalie . . . The writing of tragedies is not with Racine a cold-blooded fabrication, but the expression of the precarious character of man's life, the haunting feeling of ever-present death.

Port-Royal

But it was Port-Royal which was perhaps to play the most im-portant role in Racine's formation, and here Mauron is on solid ground. Port-Royal had been for centuries a convent of nuns near Paris. It became in the seventeenth century the centre of Jansenism, when some laymen and ecclesiastics, the so-called *Solitaires* or *Messieurs de Port-Royal*, came to live near the convent. They spent their time meditating, reading Saint Augustine and the early Fathers of the Church, writing against the Jesuits, their enemies, and also teaching young boys in small classes, the *Petites-Ecoles*. Racine was a pupil at the *Petites-Ecoles*, and Port-Royal became his home and his family. He grew up in the shadow of Jansenist theology and Jansenist morality. But his relationship with Port-Royal is more complex than that of a straight influence, for already as a youngster he was in rebellion against Port-Royal, and when he began his career in the theatre, which to Port-Royal as to English puritans was an abomination, he broke violently and publicly with his former masters. Yet he could never completely ignore or forget Port-Royal. He could never completely free himself from his childhood, and if Port-Royal had been only what he reacted against, it would still be an important element in his life.

At Port-Royal Racine lived with his grandmother and his

aunt, Sister Agnès, who was to play a decisive part at some crucial moments of his life. To the psychoanalyst Port-Royal was to Racine father and mother; it gave the child his early set of values, against which the young man and the poet rebelled. For his plays, in a way, take place inside himself before being enacted on the stage, and one of Mauron's discoveries is that there is between the situation of the characters from one play to another a recurrent pattern. One character, who may be more directly identified with the poet's ego, is rebelling against another, who claims to have rights over him, to be entitled to dictate his behaviour, and to fix his duty, while he tries to achieve what is his genuine desire: to conquer his freedom, or the woman he loves. Thus Pyrrhus desperately tries to free himself from Hermione, the fiancée to whom his ambassadors have promised his hand, and who has a right to expect him to keep his word; but it is Andromaque he loves. Néron desperately tries to free himself from the wife he was forced to marry, and even more from his domineering mother, who expects obedience from her son; but it is Junie he loves, and she becomes the symbol of his freedom. Bajazet is the prisoner of Roxane, who has power over his life, and she is ready to crown him in exchange for his love; but Bajazet loves Atalide.

The last plays show a striking change in the pattern; the Father who, in the first tragedies, is absent, or dead, or in the background, becomes an active, all-important character. Whether it is Mithridate, Agamemnon, or Thésée, he is dangerous to the Son, whom he persecutes and threatens with death. Mithridate plans to have his two sons executed. Agamemnon, in spite of his hesitations, accepts, or rather orders, the sacrifice of his daughter. Thésée curses his son, and brings upon him the wrath of a God. No father, of course, ever threatened Racine's life, and the threat is but the projection of his fear and guilt towards Port-Royal. In the Jansenist drama of *Athalie*, the father-figure of Joad is finally accepted by the Son as his guardian and protector, although the ghost of rebellion hovers in the future.

Structuralism

Goldmann as well as Mauron look for recurrent elements in Racine's theatre – in the first case the tragic vision which Racine strives, but seldom manages to achieve; in the second an ever-present pattern like the one created in a magnetic field or *champ de forces*. This pattern could be described as a structure, and structuralism has in recent years dominated literary criticism as well as linguistics, physics, mathematics, sociology, or ethnography. Structure in a static sense may be the constant pattern that determines the lasting, essential characters of a thing, be it abstract, concrete, or living. In a more dynamic sense it may also express the law that governs the perpetuation of an organism through its changes and its evolution. In Racinian criticism, structuralism is more particularly connected with the name of Roland Barthes, and his book *Sur Racine* (1963) has made use of Mauron's psychocriticism, as well as of Goldmann's sociology, and Levy-Strauss' ethnography. For M. Barthes, the main structure of Racinian theatre is a relationship of force, or authority:

A is all powerful over B
A loves B, who does not love him.

Such is the relationship of Pyrrhus and Andromaque, of Néron and Junie, of Agrippine and Néron, of Roxane and Bajazet. A trial of strength, not an emotional relationship, is therefore at the bottom of Racine's drama, and the dominant character is by definition in Barthian terminology the male one – whether he is in the play a masculine or a feminine character. R. Barthes's interpretation has aroused violent opposition, particularly from Racine's chief biographer, R. Picard. M. Barthes's style is often elliptic, paradoxical, deliberately provoking, and M. Picard occasionally scores against him. Some of his most intriguing statements, however, often convey, in a violently condensed manner, penetrating insights into our author, and Racinian criticism would be much the poorer without him.

2

The Classical Moment

A New Society

Historical periods and centuries are largely artificial divisions.
There are times, however, when history seems to accelerate,
when the old declines more swiftly, and the new asserts itself
more vigorously, and such a process seems to take place in
France in the middle of the seventeenth century. The disorderly
France of Henry IV and Louis XIII (†1643), was still an archaic
state, a feudal and clerical one, in which the aristocracy re-
tained a substantial independence, and the Church wielded
enormous influence. After 1661, when Louis XIV assumed
power, the picture was very different; a defeated, humiliated
nobility had lost all political power and much of its prestige;
the very values for which it stood, blood and race, and the
paramountcy of personal honour and personal pride were dis-
credited. The France of Louis XIV and Colbert was, relatively
speaking, a modern state, highly centralized and authoritarian.
The Court was the main artistic and literary centre, with artists
and writers more than willing to cooperate. Its life was a con-
tinual, quasi-pagan festival, with the Church (and the *dévots*
Molière was to satirize) watching in angry, impotent disap-
proval. The fact that the young King protected Molière against
his formidable enemies, and showered Racine with favours,
shows that he had more discernment and taste than was sometimes granted to him; even Lulli's music, which the King loved,
is no longer despised. At the same time, to suit the grandeur of
the King, drama and literature had to clothe themselves in
dignity, restraint, and *bienséance*, and the overwhelming splen-

dour of Versailles was to be a fitting residence to the *Grand Monarque*.

After the *Fronde*

A convenient period of transition is the protracted and destructive civil war which bears the name of the *Fronde* (1649–53), and the years that followed it. There was much in the immediate *après-guerre* that recalled the past. The poetry of Scarron, the pitiful cripple, with its amazing mixture of pathos, burlesque, and indecency, is good reading for anybody who has too simple and too noble an idea of the French seventeenth century. Madeleine de Scudéry's novels, full of love and gallantry, picturesque descriptions, and extraordinary adventures, are typical of Baroque literature; remorselessly derided by Boileau, they compare favourably with the *Three Musketeers*, and are due for early rehabilitation. Philippe Quinault, the brilliant teenager who conquered Paris with his extravagant tragi-comedies worked in the same vein. He is now of historical interest, but has already been granted, grudgingly, the merits of a good second-rater. The whole of French culture, however, was now turning its back on the Baroque. In the middle of *précieux* refinements and Baroque exuberance, Pascal's *Provinciales* (1656), burst out in France like a thunder-clap. Their immediate purpose was the defence of the Jansenist leader Antoine Arnauld, and they dealt a formidable blow at the all-powerful Society of Jesus. On the religious level they shook the facile optimism of contemporary piety, and replaced it by a much harsher, more tragic conception of man's condition. At the same time as he was denouncing the compromissions of Jesuit confessors and spiritual directors with the brutal aristocratic code of the time (it was wrong to kill, of course, but if a gentleman's honour was involved, it was a different question), Pascal was also ridiculing the far-fetched metaphors and *précieux* airs and graces which had invaded the style of catholic writers in Europe: his Jesuit fathers are memorable figures of fun. Pascal's own style was one of direct simplicity, sober, powerful eloquence, and sparkling wit. Here indeed was something radically new in the century.

Molière

Pascal died young. The true pioneer of the new age was Molière. His *Précieuses Ridicules* (1659) poked fun at the frivolous games of *précieux* society, and at the romantic, imaginative novels of the time. But Molière also laughed at other more important conventions of the time, at its stylized conception of love, at its accepted notions of heroism and devotion. Molière's comedy was what it was not because of the rules of the genre, but because Molière created it that way. To him it was more than light-hearted entertainment, and it could look tragedy in the face. Molière was quite outspoken on that subject:

> . . . il est bien plus aisé de se guinder sur de grands senti-
> ments, de braver en vers la fortune, accuser les destins, et
> dire des injures aux dieux que d'entrer comme il faut dans
> le ridicule des hommes . . .
>
> (*Critique de l'Ecole des femmes*, VI)

His contemptuous indifference towards the *doctes* and their sacred rules was another way of shaking off tradition. His first triumph, *L'Ecole des Femmes* met with enthusiasm, and also with the enmity of all traditionalists, whether religious or literary. *Tartuffe*, which touched upon ecclesiastical matters, aroused a formidable storm, which Molière only survived thanks to Louis' protection. In the year of *Tartuffe* (1664), Racine wrote his first tragedy, *La Thébaïde*.

The Classical Moment

It is in such a climate of impatience and rebellion that we must view Racine's tragedies, as one aspect of an *avant-garde* literature, discarding and rejecting the efforts that were made for so long after Racine's death to make him the standard-bearer of tradition and convention. Like Molière, if perhaps with a little less conviction, Racine scoffed at the rules. Like Molière, if in a different manner, he defied long-accepted conventions. The striking renewal of literature which is apparent in Pascal, Molière, La Fontaine, and even in Corneille's last plays, is what I shall refer to as the classical moment. There is no reason to refuse those writers an epithet with which they have been commonly associated, but the term has nothing to do with the indiscreet admiration, or blind detraction it has so often meant. It does not indicate a lack of imagination, originality, daring, genius. But it does not imply either that those writers alone follow the one and only path that could lead them to ultimate and exclusive perfection. Works that are among the greatest in world literature can well do without such intolerant adulation.

Racine and the Duke of Luynes

A social climate of disrespect encouraged by the young King himself, a disturbed childhood, and the heavy hand of Port-Royal, such are perhaps the first, basic elements in Racine's formation, not, however, the only ones. When as a fifteen-year-old youngster he came back from another Jansenist school in Beauvais, he found the *Petites-Ecoles* closed, Port-Royal in a crisis. He went to the castle of a wealthy protector of the sect, the Duke of Luynes, as a companion to the Duke's son. On the threshold of adolescence Racine found himself living in great houses among great people, who were later to protect him and to push him at Court. Their manners, their language became second nature to him, and their character was not an object of idealization, but of daily observation. When in 1663 we find him assiduously frequenting the Court at the Louvre he will be perfectly at ease there; he had neither Corneille's gaucherie nor Boileau's essentially bourgeois manners and outlook.

Racine and the Greeks

In the Duke's house the young Racine found himself working under one of the best Hellenists in France, Claude Lancelot, who was one of the *Solitaires*. This initiation to Greek was

another important element in his education. Not that his plays
are 'imitated' from Greek tragedies, as was claimed by either
naïve or disingenuous critics; except in two plays borrowed
from Euripides, Racine's actual debt to Greek sources is slight.
And it is enough to read one Greek tragedy to see the gulf that
separates it from Racine's theatre. Yet all his life, and unlike
most people of his time, Racine read Greek fluently and conceived a great and lasting love for Homer, Sophocles, Euripides.
The influence, if there was one, was at a deeper level. Greek
examples may well have encouraged Racine to a greater simplicity of style, as opposed to the tense eloquence of Corneille,
or to the conceits of *préciosité*. Also his Jansenist upbringing
helped him to understand the Greek concept of fatality. The
Greeks took him further on; Hector, the doomed hero of the
Iliad, is also its noblest figure; the terrible fate of Oedipus is not
the deserved punishment of an evil tyrant. Those the Gods
crush and destroy are not necessarily the wicked and the
damned, and the harsh severity of their fates arouse distress
and sympathy, compassion as well as awe and horror. This is
an important aspect of Racinian tragedy, and it is, perhaps, the
essence of tragedy.

Racine in Paris

Racine, as we can picture him from his uninhibited letters to
his distant cousin La Fontaine, was, when he first arrived in
Paris, a brilliant young man whose wide reading included
Latin and Greek, as well as French and Italian literature. He
was a gay companion who showed no enthusiasm for the defence
of Port-Royal, then in trouble as ever, and who in company
with his libertine cousin was 'loup avec les loups'. He was an
ambitious young man too, determined not to live the austere
life of a *Solitaire*; he had quickly understood that Port-Royal,
deeply suspect in the eyes of the government and the King,
could not, and would not, help him in his career. He had
hastened to dissociate himself from the Cause, and to address
fulsome praise to Cardinal Mazarin, to the young King, to the

new Queen, to Colbert. This keen and willing supporter, well backed by influential lords, had already been noticed at Court. And we soon find him pensioned by the King, long before he had written a single play. He was also a budding poet who could compose in honour of his sweetheart the rather vapid but not unmelodious lines of the *Stances à Parthénice*.

The First Plays: *La Thébaïde* and *Alexandre le Grand*

At the same time Racine was making his first uncertain steps as a tragic poet. *La Thébaïde ou Les Frères ennemis* is not a great play, and the extent of Racine's debt to Rotrou's tragedy, *Antigone*, can only be explained with any charity by the necessity of speed. In its original form it is an honest piece of verse writing, remarkably devoid of the musicality which is an essential aspect of Racine's poetry. But Racine must have cared for it, as he corrected it extensively at a later date, and there are numerous variants in the text. The choice of the subject, if not its dramatic treatment, is not, however, without significance. It is the story of the children of Oedipus, born of his incestuous marriage with his own mother, and particularly of his two sons. Etéocle and Polynice are the *frères ennemis*, doomed from their very birth to a violent end, who exterminate each other in the single combat that marks the climax of the drama. In this sombre play, in which none of the protagonists escape death, the Gods appear as active, malevolent wills:

> Jusques au bord du crime ils conduisent nos pas;
> Ils nous le font commettre, et ne l'excusent pas!
>
> *Théb*. III, 2

The contemporaries no doubt detected here an echo of Port-Royal's alleged predestination. But Racine's tragedy breathes aversion and rebelliousness, no humble Christian spirit of resignation. Such words, even aimed at the Gods of antiquity, were blasphemy in the seventeenth century.

Alexandre (1665), which takes us to the shores of the Hydaspes in India, was written in a much more fluent style, but

it can hardly be called a tragedy; one of the less attractive characters dies an untimely death, but the play is mainly about the
war-like and amorous triumphs of Alexander. Its facile bril-
liance took the fancy of the public and the King. It was a great
success and Racine was allowed to dedicate it to Louis. He can
hardly be blamed for writing an enthusiastic eulogy of the
French Alexander, whose favour allowed him to live the ex-
citing life of a courtier, a lover, and a fêted playwright – more
than the obscure pupil of the *Petites-Ecoles* could ever have
expected. Fate was not unkind to the pessimistic author of *La
Thébaïde*, but in fact his own capacity for happiness seems to
have been limited.

3

The New Hero

The 'Querelle d'*Andromaque*'

After *Alexandre le Grand* Racine was famous, but it is doubtful that his fame would have endured for that reason alone. *La Thébaïde* was an interesting but somewhat clumsy attempt to adapt the Greek conception of tragedy. *Alexandre* did not stray far from the traditional models of the *tragédie galante* of Quinault, and the *tragédie héroïque* of Corneille. In *Andromaque* (1667) the public unerringly detected something new in the nature of its heroes and in the very conception of tragedy, and, as to the *Ecole des Femmes* five years before, they reacted strongly, whether in a positive or a negative way. There was a 'Querelle d'*Andromaque*' as there had been a 'Querelle de *l'Ecole des Femmes*', and a 'Querelle du *Cid*'; and for the first, not the last time, the supporters of Racine and Corneille fought their confused battle.

The neatness and ingeniousness of the plot in *Andromaque*, the way in which the play develops in a perfectly natural way from the initial situation was undoubtedly one reason for its success. Pyrrhus, the son of Achilles and conqueror of Troy, has fallen in love with the widow of the greatest Trojan hero, Hector. She feels nothing but hatred for the destroyer of her city, and at the same time Pyrrhus is not free; a political marriage has been arranged between him and Hermione, daughter of the King of Sparta. The young princess has come to Pyrrhus' Court for the wedding, to which Pyrrhus cannot resolve himself. Hermione, thus publicly shamed, should have withdrawn, but she loves Pyrrhus even if he doesn't love her, and she still hopes. The deadlock is suddenly broken by the arrival of an ambassador from the Greek Kings; Oreste has come to demand the death of the child Astyanax, son of Hector and Andromaque. Pyrrhus has now a formidable weapon against Andromaque; he will save her son only if she accepts his love. Andromaque is torn between the memory of her husband and her love for her son. She now inclines one way, now the other, to the alternating joy and despair of Hermione, who unscrupulously uses the passion Oreste feels for her finally to have Pyrrhus murdered.

How confused and puzzled the spectators were is shown by the opposite criticisms levelled at the play. Some saw in Pyrrhus '*un héros à la Scudéry*', a *précieux*, romanesque hero. Others found him too brutal: '*J'avoue,*' Racine ironically commented, '*qu'il n'est pas assez résigné à la volonté de sa maîtresse, et que Céladon* a mieux connu que lui le parfait amour. Mais que faire? Pyrrhus n'avait pas lu nos romans. Il était violent de son naturel. Et tous les héros ne sont pas faits pour être des Céladons.*' Those contradictions are understandable in view of the fact that, in *Andromaque*, Racine introduced a type of tragic hero that had few, if any, models; Camille, in *Horace*, might be one, but Rodrigue, Horace, Auguste, and Polyeucte, Chimène, Emilie, and Pauline had done more to shape the traditional, i.e. the Cornelian, image of the tragic hero.

Heroism and Gallantry

As we have seen the outer form of Racine's tragedy was not very different from that of his predecessors. It was the one which the habits of the public more than the authority of the *doctes* had to some extent forced upon the authors; the three unities of time, place, and action, the *bienséance*, which forbade vulgarity of language as well as open violence or gory spectacle on the stage, which also demanded a sustained dignity of style (*unité de ton*), without comical or farcical episodes, such were the usual characters of seventeenth-century tragedy. The set speeches and soliloquies, the almost constant use of formal

---

* The devoted lover of Astrée, in Honoré d'Urfé's novel.

style, the presence of confidants, the long accounts of what the spectators were not supposed to see, increased the resemblance with traditional tragedy. More important, and more relevant to our present purpose, the characters seemed at first sight to live in the same world of love and politics, to accept the same set of values, and to acknowledge the same chivalrous code which Corneille had so magnificently restated, but which had been, since Chrétien de Troyes and the *romans courtois*, the exclusive privilege of the aristocratic or feudal classes, a code not always practised, but never disputed. It would not be difficult to illustrate this social as well as literary tradition from the plays of Racine. His princesses speak like princesses; his heroes are gallant knights, who have proved their prowess on the battlefield. Pyrrhus, the conqueror of Troy, bows in front of his 'captive', Andromaque, with consummate courtesy:

> Me cherchiez-vous, Madame?
> Un espoir si charmant me serait-il permis?
>
> *Andr.* I, 4

Oreste is ready to lead the Greeks against Epirus to avenge Hermione, as his father Agamemnon had led them against Troy to avenge Menelaus. Hermione excuses herself to her disappointed lover, Oreste, by sheltering behind her father's absolute authority:

> L'amour ne règle pas le sort d'une Princesse:
> La gloire d'obéir est tout ce qu'on nous laisse.
>
> III, 2

It would be wrong then to speak, as some nineteenth-century critics did, of the ordinariness of Racine's characters; they have inherited a long tradition of heroism and gallantry; they are proud of their elevated rank, aware of the rights and duties attached to it. Aware that the fate of Empires hangs on their decision, aware above all of that *gloire* which is the hero's ultimate concern. *Gloire* is not so much fame as the exalted feeling of pride that springs from the total freedom of those who have no masters, who are masters of themselves and masters of the world. Hermione, when she has been betrayed, knows that she owes it to herself and to her *gloire* to take revenge:

> Si je le hais, Cléone! Il y va de ma gloire.

II, 1

and from Oreste she will demand the traitor's life:

> Ne vous suffit-il pas que ma gloire offensée
> Demande une victime à moi seule adressée?

IV, 3

The denial of *gloire*

But this *gloire*, in which the hero of old fully realized himself, the Racinian hero discovers at the decisive moment that it has lost its compelling force. Sometimes, with surprise and naïve indignation, he becomes aware that the other one does not behave as he had a right to expect, that he no longer plays the game. It is not only Pyrrhus who fails Hermione, it is, she feels, all those who have led her into believing in a world of false appearances and make-believe:

> Avant qu'il me trahît, vous m'avez tous trahie.

II, 1

She had come to Epirus for the celebration of a royal wedding; six months later, slighted and humiliated, she is still waiting against her father's express order, and the proud princess will finally blackmail Oreste into murder, offering herself as a prize. Andromaque too finds it hard to believe that the gallant knight has turned blackmailer:

> L'amour peut-il si loin pousser sa barbarie?

III, 8

For Pyrrhus gives Andromaque the choice of marrying him, or watching her son die; so little is left of gallantry and respect for womanhood!

Its seem, when the play ends, that all the high ideals it first proclaimed lie in ruin, that every character has been stripped of what now looks like mere pretence, that all its values have in

fact ceased to be values. Oreste, little caring for the success of
his embassy, hoping, in fact, that it will not succeed, prepares
to carry off by force the King's fiancée (*'Oreste ravisseur!'*), and
his reason is that she will, at least, be as unhappy as himself.
The revenge to which he resolves himself in despair takes the
form not of a chivalrous duel, like that of Rodrigue in *Le Cid*,
but of a cowardly murder, in which Pyrrhus has no chance of
defending himself.

The search for authenticity

The characters in *Andromaque* are not always aware of their true
motives, even when they explain or analyse themselves. But at
essential moments and in essential decisions their choice is as
lucid as that of Corneille's heroes, and they are not, like
Romantic characters, merely carried away by the torrent of
their emotions. Pyrrhus knows full well what he is doing; in
marrying a Trojan slave, and in proclaiming her son King of
Troy, he disowns his country and his peers, undoes his own
deeds and those of Achilles his father. Oreste, when he too
abandons the path of honour and tradition, when he turns his
back to the *éthique de la gloire* does so in an explicit, deliberate act of surrender; he lucidly commits himself to blind fate:

> Je me livre en aveugle au destin qui m'entraîne.
>
> I, 1

There is a choice, then, in the Racinian hero as in the Cornelian
one, but it is not the same. Beyond honour and *gloire*, race and
blood, every character in *Andromaque* discovers in himself and
in others another reality, at first unsuspected, that denies the
validity of *gloire*. A more personal, more intimate reality. They
enter another world, unfamiliar and disquieting; they reach for
a deeper identity, and to them a more genuine one. Whereas the
first step in the Cornelian hero's self-realization, whether it be
Alidor, Rodrigue, or Polyeucte, is the mastery over his love, the
significant fact in the Racinian hero is his acceptance of a
passion that is assumed to the full, with all the mortal consequences it may entail. And whereas the ultimate goal, in

triumph or in death, is for Rodrigue, Cléopâtre, or Œdipe, the domination over all others, and the conquest of their freedom, the final realization for Oreste, Hermione, or Pyrrhus is acquiescence to a destiny, and an acknowledgement of their dependence on, of their absolute need of, another human being; Oreste cannot do without Hermione, nor Hermione without Pyrrhus, nor Pyrrhus without Andromaque.

The 'demolition of the hero'

Since the hero no longer realizes himself in the mastering of his love – or of his hatred – should we conclude from his yielding to it to his moral inadequacy, and to his unheroic character? Should we repeat the old cliché that Corneille shows the greatness of man, and Racine his weaknesses? This would be an oversimplification. No doubt we shall not find in Racine's heroes the proud ambition of independence aimed at by the Cornelian hero:

> Dans un si grand revers que vous reste-t-il?

the appalled confidant asks Médée, the murderess of her own children. 'Moi,' comes the answer, 'Moi, dis-je, et c'est assez.' In that sense, Racine and Molière shared in that process of the 'démolition du héros' (Bénichou) which seems a common trend in the classical period. In that sense Racine's heroes are antiheroes. Racine, like Molière, discarded as inhuman and probably illusory the ambition of total self-sufficiency and nondependence, as do Agnès in the *Ecole des Femmes*, or Alceste in the *Misanthrope*, or even the Cléante of *Tartuffe* ('*Les sentiments humains, mon frère, que voilà!*'). Racine, like Molière, saw as an inevitable part of our humanity our need for, and dependence on, each other.

The new hero

For the rejection of the Cornelian ideal – which Corneille was later to reject himself in a dramatic way – does not simply mean weakness, lack of courage or fortitude. It does not make

Racine's characters mediocre, average men, with the petty
fears and rash impulses of the average man, with his timorous-
ness and conformity. They accept risks, and pay the price. With
their life they will pay for something that is obviously to them
more precious than life. Amoral Racine's sinister heroes may
be, since they free themselves from traditional values and
deliberately reject traditional morality, but not weak. How the
poet made tragedy out of such characters does not concern us
here, and we shall come to it in another chapter. One more of
those characters we should examine now, the central one in the
play, Andromaque.

Andromaque's dilemma

Andromaque's attitude towards *gloire* is even more extraordinary and more revealing than that of the other characters.
She is not guilty of murder or blackmail, and her concern is not
for the destruction but for the saving of a life. Yet she is not
without passion. Andromaque is in fact ruled by two passions
which are in a strange way contradictory and identical: her
husband and her son, Hector and Astyanax. She cannot accept
Pyrrhus' love because she still belongs body and soul to her
dead husband, and because Pyrrhus is the son of Achilles, who
killed Hector, and also because she is a Trojan, and he is a
Greek and the destroyer of her city. Pyrrhus now wishes to
forget it, wishes to forget the massacres and the dead, but she
cannot:

> Dois-je les oublier, s'il ne s'en souvient plus?
> Dois-je oublier Hector privé de funérailles,
> Et traîné sans honneur autour de nos murailles?
> Dois-je oublier son père à mes pieds renversé,
> Ensanglantant l'autel qu'il tenait embrassé?
>
> III, 8

But if Andromaque cannot accept Pyrrhus it is unthinkable that
she might reject him, for her son's life is in his hands; he can as
he pleases save him, or deliver him to the Greeks, who clamour
for his death. Surely Andromaque cannot lose all that is left to
her of Troy. And she cannot let him die because through a

mysterious transfer Astyanax has taken the place of her dead husband; he *is* the princely hero she has lost:

> Il m'aurait tenu lieu d'un père et d'un époux.
>
> I, 4

Andromaque says, strangely enough, of the child. And when she holds him in her arms:

> C'est Hector, disait-elle en l'embrassant toujours;
> Voilà ses yeux, sa bouche, et déjà son audace;
> C'est lui-même, c'est toi, cher époux, que j'embrasse.
>
> II, 5

To her beloved son, Pyrrhus offers his life, freedom, a crown, and the prospect of a new Troy:

> Votre Ilion encor peut sortir de sa cendre;
> Je puis, en moins de temps que les Grecs ne l'ont pris,
> Dans ses murs relevés couronner votre fils.
>
> I, 4

No lover of *gloire* could ask for more; the naïve Céphise, Andromaque's confidant, is jubilant. But Andromaque cares nothing for *gloire*:

> Seigneur, tant de grandeurs ne nous touchent plus guère: (. . .)
> A de moindres faveurs des malheureux prétendent,
> Seigneur: c'est un exil que mes pleurs vous demandent.
> Souffrez que loin des Grecs, et même loin de vous,
> J'aille cacher mon fils et pleurer mon époux.
>
> I, 4

Baroque and Classicism

Here is indeed an entirely new type of hero. There is in Andromaque none of the ambiguity we still find in Hermione, Pyrrhus, and Oreste. *Gloire* has been totally devalued. The contemporaries were aware of the novelty, although they expressed it in a narrow, even trivial manner, and chose to see in it no more than the rivalry of two men. The parallel between Racine and Corneille was to remain for three centuries one of the favourite sports of French critics, but there is much more to that conflict than Racine's refusal to write Cornelian plays, more than the clash of two men. In a social, historical perspective the new drama and the new hero testify to the decline of aristocracy and aristocratic values that followed the resounding defeat of the nobility in the *Fronde*. In a moral, religious context it does appear as a chapter in the progressive destruction of the hero as superman carried out in different ways by Pascal and the Jansenists, as well as by Molière and Racine. In a broad cultural sense it marks a decisive break with Baroque art and Baroque style, which had dominated Europe for a century, as well as with the values that held sway since the time of the Counter-Reformation. But the conflict in *Andromaque* remains significant even if it is abstracted from its immediate historical context, and the various interpretations of the play complete and recoup each other rather than contradict each other. To C. Mauron, Pyrrhus's refusal to conform to the traditional values of the tragic hero expresses Racine's own rebellion against the rigid standards of Port-Royal. Another critic observes that in *Andromaque* we see the revenge of Troy against her Greek enemies. In an even more general way Roland Barthes sees in it the victory of the future over the past.

Old values and new values

In whichever light *Andromaque* is considered it seems to be a rebellious, even a revolutionary play that illustrates the destruction of established values and the established order. In the play the spokesman of this established order would, at first sight, appear to be Oreste, ambassador, who at the very beginning of the play reminds Pyrrhus of his duty to Greece, and of the great memory of his father, Achilles. When Pyrrhus rejects those claims, Oreste draws the inevitable conclusion:

> Ainsi la Grèce en vous trouve un enfant rebelle ?
>
> I, 2

a conclusion which will be confirmed by Pyrrhus himself:

Tous les Grecs conjurés fondaient sur un rebelle.

II, 5

But we know that Oreste, precisely, is only a spokesman, that he secretly hopes for his embassy to fail. Hermione is the one who fiercely defends the established order which she embodies in herself. Hermione is Pyrrhus' fiancée, sent to Epirus by her father's order, a token of the pledge exchanged by two mighty Kings. ('*Par mes ambassadeurs mon cœur vous fut promis*'.) She is the Greek princess to whom Pyrrhus has given as a rival a Trojan slave, '*Etrangère . . . que dis-je, esclave dans l'Epire*', as Pyrrhus himself describes Andromaque in a moment o anger. Hermione has on her side Duty, Honour, Country, and the Gods, guardians and guarantors of oaths. The fact that she is not a passive or detached spectator does not imply that the order Hermione constantly invokes in her defence is in any way an alibi; it only serves to compound and multiply her anger and indignation at the wrong she is suffering. She is, as Roland Barthes puts it '*le gage d'une société tout entière . . . en sorte que rompre la fidélité à Hermione, c'est rejeter à la fois le Père, le Passé, la Patrie, et la Religion*'.

Judged by those standards Pyrrhus is indeed the rebel, and as Hermione never tires of repeating it, *le parjure, le perfide, le traître*. All her insults he deserves, as much as Néron will deserve those of Agrippine. We can, of course, blandly assume that it would be more moral – more consistent with established morality – for Pyrrhus to keep his word to Hermione, and to connive at the murder of a child who is, after all, only a slave, and the son of an enemy. He would be more immediately recognizable as a hero if he agreed to give that infallible proof of his heroic essence: to conquer his passion, and sacrifice his love. But Racine's play does not encourage such easy taking of sides and such facile generalization. If Hermione is the old order, Pyrrhus is the breaking away from it, and the attempt at creating a new one. What Pyrrhus asks from Andromaque is that she should forget her Trojan past, in which she is as firmly fixed as Hermione in her conviction of Right, that she should accept that there is a future for her. This tremendous step Andro-

maque finally agrees to take, at least for her son, for she sees no
future for herself but death. For the child, however, she accepts
the abolition of the past and the rebirth of hope:

> Si tu vivais pour moi, vis pour le fils d'Hector.
> De l'espoir des Troyens seule dépositaire,
> Songe à combien de rois tu deviens nécessaire.
>
> IV, 1

she tells her confidant, adding the decisive message:

> Mais qu'il ne songe plus, Céphise, à nous venger.

Pyrrhus's' death, therefore, in saving her life saves more than
her life. Out of Pyrrhus's love for Andromaque, and Andromaque's love for her son, there is born at least the outline of a
new order; a Trojan princess is accepted as Queen of a Greek
city; the son of Hector, one day, perhaps, will succeed the son
of Achilles. The old order is denied, just as it was denied by
Horace and Agnès in *L'Ecole des Femmes*. It vanishes with its
old loyalties and its old hatreds. Hermione publicly killing
herself over the body of another woman's husband, Oreste
tearing himself to shreds in self-doubt and self-condemnation
both testify to its defeat, as indeed does the headlong flight of
the Greeks, no longer avengers of Right, but criminals against
whom a whole nation is aroused:

> Tout le peuple assemblé nous poursuit à main-forte.
> Aux ordres d'Andromaque ici tout est soumis.
>
> V, 5

Les Plaideurs

Fresh from the success of *Andromaque* Racine wrote the following year (1668) his only comedy, *Les Plaideurs*. This is a witty,
brilliant piece of entertainment, and the acrobatics of its
dazzling versification antedate by one hundred and fifty years
those of Victor Hugo. It tells without any concern for *vraisem-
blance* the extravagant story of a crazy judge, Perrin Dandin,
who wants to pass sentences at all times of the day and night.
To keep him quiet at home his son lets him preside over the
mock trial of a dog who has stolen a chicken. The farcical

figures of the litigants – the *plaideurs* – Chicaneau and the Comtesse de Pimbesche, as crazy as their judge, pop in and out of this unlikely plot, into which a thin romantic story is also woven. The characters are two-dimensional, and the play never approaches the level of Molière. It offers opportunities for social satire aimed at the ignorance and verbose eloquence of the barristers, and at the incompetence and cruelty of the judges. To a young girl Dandin offers the spectacle of torture:

Bon! cela fait toujours passer une heure ou deux.

Plaid. III, 4

More surprisingly it also reveals Racine as a political satirist. Colbert trying to protect the public from some of the worst abuses of French justice, its corruption and dilatoriness, had promulgated new edicts which, naturally enough, proved most unpopular with the law people. It is significant that Racine brings up the same accusations against them, thus holding to ridicule the minister's opponents.

4

The Racinian Prince

Britannicus (1669)

The main conflict in *Britannicus* is between the mother and the son, between the Empress Agrippine and the very young Emperor Néron. Agrippine has with ruthless single-mindedness put her son on the Imperial throne after murdering her husband, the Emperor Claudius, but she never meant to give up the reality of power. Néron, tired of being Emperor only in name, is increasingly rebellious against his domineering mother. Furious, Agrippine imagines to remind him of his dependence by supporting the young son of Claudius, Britannicus, the legitimate heir to the throne: she will allow him to marry Junie, an Imperial Princess and a descendant of Augustus. Néron's answer is to have the girl arrested in the middle of the night, and imprisoned in his palace. So far the conflict has been purely political, a trial of force between the mother and the son, but none of these characters are merely pieces in a chess game. Junie and Britannicus have loved each other ever since they were children; their separation is to them heart-breaking. Nor is Néron insensitive: his mother has married him to a woman for whom he has never felt anything. The sudden appearance of Junie is to him a revelation of love and beauty, of himself, and of the possibility of happiness. We also discover that his possessive mother Agrippine is jealous of this new love; she wants him to have a wife he does not love . . . To the conflict between Agrippine and Néron is now added one between Néron and Britannicus, rivals for the crown as well as for the girl. As there can only be one Emperor in Rome, the fight is fought to a finish, and Britannicus finally goes down, poisoned by his rival in a scene of mock reconciliation.

This is the end of the play, but only the beginning of Néron's murderous career, and the tragedy can be described in Racine's words as the birth of a monster. We must guard, however, against the temptations of making Néron a personification of Evil: Racine does not deal in such dreary abstractions. Even though he wrote in his preface with his usual, sarcastic banter that Néron was 'un très méchant homme', he is not essentially more wicked than Pyrrhus, Oreste, or in *Bajazet*, Roxane, and his scruples, hesitations, oscillations are portrayed with as much delicacy as in any other Racinian hero.

It would be easy to find in *Britannicus* the same indifference to conventions, the same fundamental negation of values as in *Andromaque*. Junie, concerned mainly with the life and safety of her Prince, cares as little for the pomp and power of Empire as Andromaque for the restoration of Troy and the crowning of her son. And *Britannicus* no doubt is like *Andromaque* a tragedy of love and passion. But it is also, to a much greater extent than *Andromaque*, a political tragedy, and it is in the political attitudes which it illustrates that the rebellion against, and rejection of, accepted values appear most clearly. Ch. Mauron already noted the similarity of pattern in *Andromaque* and in *Britannicus*, especially in the situation of Pyrrhus between Andromaque and Hermione, and that of Néron between Junie and Agrippine. Both are attracted to a gentler, more loving type of woman who, in both cases, rejects them. And both are trying to escape from a more violent, more possessive woman who stands on her rights, whether it is Hermione, the possessive fiancée, or Agrippine, the possessive mother. But it is also possible to note another recurrent trait in the two plays. There is at a very great depth a conflict between what is, and what tries to be, between a certain order that strives to persist, and another one that attempts to be born. In *Britannicus* these two conceptions of politics are clearly expounded by two anti-thetic characters, the traditional, moral conception by Burrhus, the amoral, Machiavellian one that finally prevails by Narcisse.

Between them Néron dramatically oscillates, before making his momentous choice.

Morals and politics

Burrhus stands for the respect of the law, and for the past. He rejoices in seeing in the first happy years of Néron's reign the people elect their magistrates, and the Senate, the traditional seat of power in the old Republic, regain its influence and prestige. These institutions have in the past guaranteed Roman freedom; they have been tried and proved for centuries; they have become respectable because they have been respected for so long, and in the eyes of Burrhus they stand for genuine values. To him political values go hand in hand with social and family values, with the sacredness of natural ties between mother and son, or between brother and brother. Such absolute values are binding on everyone, and not least on the Monarch who is, or should be, to his subjects a trusted father, finding his own safety and happiness in their love. Burrhus is loyal to his Emperor, whose rights he defends against the encroachments of his mother. But he is stricken with grief and despair when he learns of Néron's intention of getting rid of his adoptive brother, Britannicus. Such a deed of blood will only alienate his subjects, infuriate the young Prince's partisans, and start an endless chain of murders and vendettas, with Néron as its ultimate victim. It is bad politics and bad morality: it is bad politics, he says, *because* it is bad morality:

> (. . .) si de vos flatteurs vous suivez la maxime,
> Il vous faudra, Seigneur, courir de crime en crime,
> Soutenir vos rigueurs par d'autres cruautés,
> Et laver dans le sang vos bras ensanglantés.
> Britannicus mourant excitera le zèle
> De ses amis, tout prêts à prendre sa querelle.
> Ces vengeurs trouveront de nouveaux défenseurs,
> Qui, même après leur mort, auront des successeurs.
> Vous allumez un feu qui ne pourra s'éteindre.
> Craint de tout l'univers, il vous faudra tout craindre,

Toujours punir, toujours trembler dans vos projets,
Et pour vos ennemis compter tous vos sujets.

Brit. IV, 3

Narcisse and the Racinian Prince

In the face of such admirable sentiments, it is tempting to
dismiss Narcisse as a mere foil and a black villain, but the
temptation must be resisted: *Britannicus* goes deeper and further than a childish duel between 'goodies' and 'baddies'. The
people the ruler must deal with, Narcisse says, are not a society
of starry-eyed men of good will; they are a mob, selfish, violent,
dominated by elementary instincts, and if those instincts are not
harshly contained the only result will be anarchy, the war of all
against all, and with it general insecurity, and the end of
civilized society. The ruler's role, therefore, is not to pander to
the absurd, sometimes destructive, caprices of the mob; it is to
rule, not to be ruled. It is to enforce order, which the people
need for their own good, but are unable to create by themselves.
If the Prince asserts his will, the common herd will be only too
pleased to obey, for that is its secret wish, and it is as cowardly
and servile as it is loud-mouthed and arrogant when indulged:

Et prenez-vous, Seigneur, leurs caprices pour guides?
Avez-vous prétendu qu'ils se tairaient toujours?
Est-ce à vous de prêter l'oreille à leurs discours?
De vos propres désirs perdrez-vous la mémoire?
Et serez-vous le seul que vous n'oserez croire?
Mais, Seigneur, les Romains ne vous sont pas connus.
Non, non, dans leurs discours ils sont plus retenus.
Tant de précaution affaiblit votre règne:
Ils croiront, en effet, mériter qu'on les craigne.
Au joug depuis longtemps ils se sont façonnés:
Ils adorent la main qui les tient enchaînés.

IV, 4

Law and order, the security of the State, on which everything
depends, welfare, justice, and morality itself, must therefore be
preserved at all costs and by all means. In an absolute monarchy like that of Imperial Rome, or Bourbon France, the
security of the State is based on the security of the Monarch.

All that threatens the Prince threatens the State; all that strengthens the Prince is in the interest of the State, and for the common good. The Reason of State must prevail over all other considerations, it justifies every deed, every crime, for then it ceases to be a crime. *Britannicus* is not a *pièce à thèse*, and we should not try to identify Racine with either Narcisse or Burrhus. We can see that he has extracted a maximum of pathos from the harsh doctrine of the Reason of State, whose victims are the young and charming Britannicus as well as the loving, lucid Junie, and their common disaster is meant to arouse sympathy. But is it true to say, as Burrhus does, that Britannicus is an innocent victim of calumny, that he is no enemy of his brother? The truth is that Britannicus hates Néron, that he sees him as the usurper of a crown that belongs to him, as he tells him to his face, that with the complicity of Agrippine he is plotting the death of Néron, which is the only way for him to regain the throne and the possession of Junie.

What then is Néron to do? Is it sheer wickedness to defend his throne and his life? For one cannot be saved without the other. Is there any other way open to him? There is Burrhus' way: compromise; Néron will keep the crown, Britannicus the girl. This is a good, sensible solution. But in the cold, objective light of history it is unlikely that Néron or Britannicus could ever trust each other and live in peace. Not only their past, and the blood of the murdered Emperor, Britannicus' father, but the treacherous intrigues of Agrippine, and her own limitless ambition made peaceful coexistence between the two Emperors, the usurper and the pretender, impossible. One of them, one day, would strike. Néron struck first. Viewed from a purely political point of view, the only possible conclusion one may draw from the play is that Burrhus' political system is a pipe dream, and that Narcisse alone has assessed the situation correctly. Politics aim at success, and success has its rules and its price, as Racine harshly reminds us. Whether it is worth the price is another matter.

Bérénice (1670)

Rome is as present, and the Reason of State, it seems, plays as powerful a role in *Bérénice* as in *Britannicus*. Titus has just succeeded his father, the Emperor Vespasian, whose splendid funeral Bérénice recalls in unforgettable lines:

> De cette nuit, Phénice, as-tu vu la splendeur?
> Tes yeux ne sont-ils pas tout pleins de sa grandeur?
> Ces flambeaux, ce bûcher, cette nuit enflammée,
> Ces aigles, ces faisceaux, ce peuple, cette armée,
> Cette foule de rois, ces consuls, ce sénat,
> Qui tous de mon amant empruntaient leur éclat;
> Cette pourpre, cet or, que rehaussait sa gloire,
> Et ces lauriers encor témoins de sa victoire.
>
> *Bér.* I, 5

Ever hostile to Kings and foreigners, Rome views with suspicion the projected marriage of Titus with Bérénice, Queen of Palestine, and it is finally to Rome, it seems, that Titus sacrifices Bérénice and his love. Rather than violate a fundamental law of the Empire, Titus, the guardian of its laws, the first magistrate of Rome, prefers to follow the austere examples set by those Romans of old, Regulus, Manlius, Brutus, who, a century after Racine's death, were to be so prominent in neo-classical art and revolutionary rhetoric:

> L'un, jaloux de sa foi, va chez les ennemis
> Chercher, avec la mort, la peine toute prête;
> D'un fils victorieux l'autre proscrit la tête;
> L'autre, avec des yeux secs et presque indifférents,
> Voit mourir ses deux fils par son ordre expirants.
>
> IV, 5

At the end of the play the two lovers part for ever, a shining example of devotion to duty, and an unexpectedly Cornelian dénouement to a Racinian tragedy . . . *if* that is really what Racine meant to do.

If we consider the play from a purely political point of view, it is immediately clear that the Reason of State here means something quite different from what it meant in *Britannicus*. It is no longer the instrument as well as the justification of the

Prince's *bon plaisir*. It is an abstract law, which compels the Prince as well as his subjects. In Néron's mind the murder of Britannicus should establish beyond all doubt who is the ruler of Rome, as well as rid him of a dangerous rival, humble Agrippine, *and* give him Junie, to whose love his supreme rank gives him some kind of right. From Titus, Reason of State exacts a sacrifice which is to him greater than that of his life itself, a kind of oblation of himself. A second point, and a puzzling one, is that Racine, far from stating the cruel dilemma of his hero with the maximum of clarity and force, seems on the contrary to veil and to dilute it: Titus bows to Roman law, but in *Bérénice* as in *Britannicus*, the Prince *is* the Law, and no one claims to oppose his absolute will:

> Vous pouvez tout: aimez, cessez d'être amoureux,
> La cour sera toujours du parti de vos vœux.
>
> II, 2

It is the irrational fury of the mob rather than the majesty of Roman law Titus seems to fear, but, as he says himself, all is quiet in Rome:

> Car enfin Rome a-t-elle expliqué ses souhaits?
> L'entendons-nous crier autour de ce palais? (. . .)
> Tout se tait.
>
> IV, 4

That elusive duty, those arguments that dissolve as soon as one tries to state them, that perpetual reticence of *Bérénice* have embarrassed and irritated critics, except those who firmly took the Cornelian *débat* at its face value, although they missed the imperious, exalting accent of Cornelian heroism. Others expressed impatience at the flimsiness of the subject: Boileau squarely asserted that this was no material for a tragedy, but fortunately Racine did not take advice from Boileau; Racine's own son found *Bérénice* ridiculous; some, like Sainte-Beuve, admired it as a minor play, an elegy rather than a tragedy. Could it be that the solution of the enigma is not in the politics of the play?

Bajazet (1672)

Bajazet offers a clearer message. The political struggle is between the ferocious Sultan Mourad IV, Amurat, as Racine calls him, who has already ordered the execution of his younger brother Bajazet as a potential rival, but who never appears on the stage, and on the other hand his Grand Vizier, Acomat, who has fallen from favour for obscure reasons, perhaps because as a victorious general he gave umbrage to his terrible master. Acomat is, even more than Narcisse, and without Narcisse's black villainy, the exponent of explicit Machiavellian politics. Acomat knows full well that the Prince 'must destroy those who can do him harm, and are likely to do so'; he knows that

> une mort sanglante est l'unique traité
> Qui reste entre l'esclave et le maître irrité.
>
> *Baj.* IV, 7

He therefore plots the downfall of the reigning Sultan, who would be replaced by Bajazet. He has cleverly allowed the Sultana, whom Amurat has entrusted with power in his absence, to catch a glimpse of her youthful prisoner: Roxane has fallen in love with him, and is ready to betray the Sultan and have Bajazet proclaimed in Constantinople: she only asks that Bajazet should make her sovereign, and elevate her above the concubines of the harem, that he should marry her. Meanwhile Acomat has worked on popular feeling in the capital (popular uproars often play their part in Racine's tragedies); he counts on Bajazet's popularity with the army. He has also secured the support of the religious leaders:

> Pour moi, j'ai su déjà par mes brigues secrètes
> Gagner de notre loi les sacrés interprètes:
> Je sais combien crédule en sa dévotion
> Le peuple suit le frein de la religion.
>
> I, 2

These were daring lines in the seventeenth century, even when ostensibly applied to an alien religion, and reflected the thought of the French admirers of Machiavelli and the 'libertins'. There

is a difficulty which Acomat, with all his intelligence, finds hard
to comprehend: because Bajazet does not love Roxane, he is
reluctant to give the required promise. To Acomat the way out
is clear:

> Promettez. Affranchi du péril qui vous presse,
> Vous verrez de quel poids sera votre promesse!

And when Bajazet protests:

> Ne rougissez point. Le sang des Ottomans
> Ne doit point en esclave obéir aux serments.
> Consultez ces héros que le droit de la guerre
> Mena victorieux jusqu'au bout de la terre:
> Libres dans leur victoire, et maîtres de leur foi,
> L'intérêt de l'Etat fut leur unique loi;
> Et d'un trône si saint la moitié n'est fondée
> Que sur la foi promise et rarement gardée.

> II, 3

'Those princes who achieved great things', Machiavelli said,
'are those who cared little to keep their promise . . . It is
enough that the Prince should be victorious and preserve the
State'.

Yet in spite of his careful plans Acomat's design comes to
nothing. Bajazet is unable to feign passion for Roxane because
he loves Atalide, and if, at her request, he consents to allow the
Sultana to persist in her error, Atalide herself is unable to
control her jealousy when she believes she has convinced him.
Whereas true Machiavellism is an attempt to bring under the
control of rationality man's impulses and passions, it is, in
Bajazet, the blind, obscure forces of love, hatred, desire,
jealousy that lead Bajazet, Roxane, and Atalide. Acomat remains outside the real drama; he is in fact the only one who
will escape with his life, and his final departure is none too
dignified: his friends still need him, he says; he will

> Défendre jusqu'au bout leurs jours qu'ils m'ont commis.

> V, 11

Under Roxane's orders Bajazet is strangled by the *muets*,
those executioners of the Sultan's whose tongue had been cut

off to ensure their discretion. Atalide commits suicide, blaming herself for the death of her lover. Roxane is executed by order of the Sultan, who apparently was all the time aware of her plots.

The Reason of State then appears triumphant in *Bajazet* as well as in *Britannicus*, but in a different way: at the end of *Britannicus* Néron is in despair because he has for ever lost Junie, but politically he has prevailed not only over Britannicus but over Agrippine, a much more formidable adversary, because he has outplayed her in dissimulation and ruthlessness. *Bajazet* confirms the same truth, of which Racine gives the counterproof: its three heroes perish because all are dominated or blinded by passion, because they waste priceless hours in deadly quarrels, piques, and delays, while the Sultan's messenger is galloping towards his capital – one of many examples in which Racine used to dramatic effect the narrow limits of time which tradition allowed to tragedy.

Politics are never absent from seventeenth-century tragedy: they are part of its definition. But Racine's peculiar brand of politics, and the importance he accords to the Reason of State belong to him alone: Corneille, at least in his early plays, and like most of his contemporaries, goes out of his way to reject it. In Racine it will be found in Mithridate, in the Ulysse and the Agamemnon of *Iphigénie*, even in the two formidable protagonists of his sacred drama of *Athalie*: Joad and Athalie herself. It did not change greatly, even if Racine's attitude to it must have changed. The harsh, the bitter truth which the young author of *Britannicus* compelled his reluctant audience to contemplate, impatiently brushing aside what to him was feeble delusion, he later viewed no doubt with fear and despair; after the return to Port-Royal and Jansenism it must have stood in the eyes of the ageing Racine as the inescapable proof of fallen man's incapacity of achieving good in this world, and as a constant reminder of original sin.

5

The New Tragedy

Aristotle's *Poetics*

What is a tragedy, and what is it that makes it tragic? Perhaps we may start with the definition given by Aristotle twenty-three centuries ago in his *Poetics*, as it was well known to seventeenth-century writers, and to Racine. Aristotle first emphasizes what he calls the seriousness of tragedy, its gravity, dignity, solemnity; perhaps he over-emphasizes it, for there are familiar scenes, and even humour, in Sophocles or Euripides. He also notes its aesthetic character: tragedy shuns realism and triviality: it uses not only verse, but song as well as music and dance. Perhaps the most important and the most pregnant passage of Aristotle is the one in which he defines tragedy by the effect it should produce upon the spectator: fear and pity, terror and compassion. This presupposes towards the hero a feeling of sympathy, so that the spectator suffers with him, and sorrows at his misfortune. It excludes the play that ends with the downfall of an abominable tyrant, the play of retribution in which, to universal applause, the guilty hero receives his just punishment. Such vindictive or self-complacent feelings are not tragic feelings, and Aristotle specified that the hero should be neither a man of exceptional virtue nor an utter villain; he should be a man 'like ourselves', neither a saint nor a devil – not, though, any 'man in the street', but one who has won fame and found happiness. And he must fall into misfortune not through some vice or depravity but through 'an error', a mistaken judgement, a faulty intuition, a wrong decision, such as no man who is not a superman can avoid. Only by such self-identification with the suffering hero, by the feeling that 'here but for the grace of God go I' could the onlooker go through the tragic experience, and, as in a sudden revelation, perceive the precariousness of all human happiness and the severity of our fate. But he would now contemplate it in a poignant, yet in a more detached, more serene mood, and in this final *catharsis* the unbearable passions of terror and pity would then be sublimated or *purified*.

Aristotle in the seventeenth century

It is remarkable that the seventeenth-century *doctes*, who wrote volumes on Aristotle, misunderstood him on some essential points.* Corneille's misunderstanding was the wilful misunderstanding of the creator and the genius. In his *Discours* and *Examens*, by far the best dramatic criticism of the century, he politely refers to Aristotle's tragic emotions of pity and fear, and blandly adds a third one which makes nonsense of them: admiration. There are of course in Corneille's plays tragic potentialities, tragic moments, in which the hero's happiness or his life are threatened. But we identify with his final triumph, not with his tragic downfall. Rodrigue or Auguste are heroes because they conquer their passions and their fears as well as their opponents. Corneille never lets us forget that they belong to an aristocracy of birth and blood which is by nature far above the common man. Polyeucte is not a man who is neither wholly good nor wholly bad, as Aristotle said, but, as Corneille proudly claimed, a man without any weakness, a saint.

Tragedies of admiration or retribution, tragicomedies in name or in fact, with a happy ending, make up the greatest part of seventeenth-century dramatic literature, whereas even if Racine did not borrow or copy his subjects from Greek tragedies, it could be said that rather than with Jodelle, Garnier, Corneille, he seems to link hands with Aeschylus, Sophocles, and Euripides (André Bonnard). But his relation with them is one of filiation, not imitation, and his careful reading of the *Poetics*, which he partly translated, resulted not in the mechanical applications of 'rules' but in an entirely new crea-

* On the rules they extracted from Aristotle see p. 21

tion, in which, like seeds in a new soil, old ideas took up a new form and a new life.

There was one reason among many others why Greek tragedy had been an unsuitable model for the baroque writers of seventeenth-century France: it went against deeply held religious beliefs as well as ingrained prejudices and habits of mind. For tragedy does not just tell a story about particular individuals; it has a universal value; as Aristotle put it, it is more philosophic than history; it tells of man's condition, and offers exemplary situations. It was impossible for a pious catholic of 1640 to tell of a noble hero struck by a vengeful God: it was an insult to divine justice, a negation of Providence. Only rebellious 'libertins' like Théophile had done it. But Racine too was a rebel.

The Greek filiation

The link with Greek tragedy appears perhaps more clearly in his first, imperfect play, *La Thébaïde*, in which the heroes are the sons of Oedipus, the *frères ennemis*, Etéocle and Polynice. They are rivals for their father's crown, and they end by murdering each other, but their hatred is not a result of their ambition; it has a supernatural origin: it is the curse of the Gods upon the sons of the incest, for the Gods punish Oedipus *and* the sons of Oedipus for the crime they have compelled him to commit, as Jocaste, his mother and his wife, bitterly reminds us:

> (. . .) ô Dieux, un crime involontaire
> Devait-il attirer toute votre colère?
> Le connaissais-je, hélas! ce fils infortuné?
> Vous-même dans mes bras vous l'avez amené.
> C'est vous dont la rigueur m'ouvrit ce précipice.
> Voilà de ces grands Dieux la suprême justice!
> Jusques au bord du crime ils conduisent nos pas;
> Ils nous le font commettre, et ne l'excusent pas!
> Prennent-ils donc plaisir à faire des coupables,
> Afin d'en faire après d'illustres misérables?
>
> *Théb*. III, 2

There is a very definite echo of this kind of tragedy in *Andromaque*, in the role of Oreste. God, says Oreste, it is an unjust God, 'une injuste puissance', who, from his very birth, had

elected him, like the sons of Oedipus, as the object of His
hatred, who tortured him for His pleasure; to the divine curse
Oreste in his final words answers himself with a curse, the more
blasphemous for its biting irony:

> Grâce aux Dieux! Mon malheur passe mon espérance:
> Oui, je te loue, ô Ciel, de ta persévérance.
> Appliqué sans relâche au soin de me punir,
> Au comble des douleurs tu m'as fait parvenir.
> Ta haine a pris plaisir à former ma misère;
> J'étais né pour servir d'exemple à ta colère,
> Pour être du malheur un exemple accompli.
> Hé bien! je meurs content, et mon sort est rempli.
>
> *Andr.* V, 5

'Like flies to wanton boys, so are we to the Gods,' Shakespeare said in a sombre moment, in *King Lear*, 'They kill us for
their sport.' But in catholic France the Greek idea of amoral,
ambivalent Gods, life-givers and life-destroyers, bountiful and
cruel like Nature itself, was an alien conception that could not
really be transplanted in a modern play. What came more
readily to French minds was the Calvinistic doctrine of predestination, which the Jansenists were accused of sharing, and
this is the justification of those who wish to see in Racine's
theatre the illustration of Jansenism. But a hidden God without
the notion of man's Fall, without a personal feeling of guilt,
without humility, resignation, and love is more akin to seventeenth-century 'libertinage', or free-thought, than to any form
of Christianity. The origin of Racine's tragic vision in his
education, in his childhood, in his unconscious, is one thing;
his tragic vision itself is another. Racine's theatre is neither
Jansenist nor a mere reshuffling of Greek tragedy: in both
cases the action of God or the Gods would have to be given a
fundamental importance and be stated explicitly, as will be the
case in *Athalie*. What we have instead in the plays which follow
La Thébaïde is a gradual elimination of the divine, transcendent
element. From this point of view *Andromaque* is still a play of
transition, which preserves not a few characters of *La Thébaïde*.
In *Britannicus* the new kind of tragedy Racine is creating ap-

pears with much greater clarity, and to understand it we must
go back to the nature of its political conflict, which is dominated
by the Reason of State.

The new tragedy

No one would make the Reason of State into a God, yet it
has for all the actors in the drama a very real and very terrible
existence. It is made of a combination of objective and sub-
jective factors, of a tangle of psychological, social, political,
historical elements which cannot be altered, and which assumes
the nature of a blind, natural law without any moral character: it plays the part of the ancient Fate. Britannicus' name, his
birth, his rights as the legitimate heir of a throne and as the son
of the slain Emperor, his youthful pride, to say nothing of
Agrippine's intrigues, make it impossible for him, without
losing his very identity, not to try and regain a crown which he
firmly believes to be his. On the other hand his youth and in-
experience – he is fifteen, Racine says – his lack of any trusted
adviser, his isolation, which has been carefully engineered by
Agrippine since the time when he was a child, his own nature,
which is of an open, generous disposition, make it impossible
that he should win the contest. Britannicus cannot win a battle
which he cannot decline to fight.

Néron's dilemma is just as severe. Even without his jealousy,
which acts as a catalyst and quickens the pace of the conflict,
Néron cannot allow the presence of a pretender who has left
him in no doubt that he considers him a usurper; the very walls
of the Imperial palace, Britannicus tells Néron,

> ne nous ont pas vus l'un et l'autre élever,
> Moi pour vous obéir, et vous pour me braver.
>
> *Brit.* III, 8

When with the help of Agrippine, Britannicus and 'la moitié du
Sénat' plot against his throne and his life. Néron cannot afford
to remain passive. But on the other hand, not only will the
killing of Britannicus trigger off the chain of murders which
Burrhus has forecast, but the very act of a preventive execution,
the fact that Néron, watching the spasms of agony of his adop-

tive brother, can preserve a calm, unconcerned countenance dehumanizes him, and makes him the 'monster' he was not before. It will eventually lead him to his own, violent death, and in destroying him as a human being, it makes him pay as dear a price perhaps as Britannicus.

> Néron l'a vu mourir sans changer de couleur,

Burrhus says, a horrified witness of Britannicus' death.

> Ses yeux indifférents ont déjà la constance
> D'un tyran dans le crime endurci dès l'enfance.
>
> V, 7

As for Agrippine she cannot be understood unless we accept the reality of her love for her son, however possessive, selfish, and domineering this love may have been.

> Dès vos plus jeunes ans, mes soins et mes tendresses
> N'ont arraché de vous que de feintes caresses.
> Rien ne vous a pu vaincre; et votre dureté
> Aurait dû dans son cours arrêter ma bonté.
> Que je suis malheureuse! Et par quelle infortune
> Faut-il que tous mes soins me rendent importune?
> Je n'ai qu'un fils. O Ciel, qui m'entends aujourd'hui,
> T'ai je fait quelques vœux qui ne fussent pour lui?
> Remords, crainte, périls, rien ne m'a retenue; (. . .)
> J'ai fait ce que j'ai pu: vous régnez, c'est assez.
> Avec ma liberté, que vous m'avez ravie,
> Si vous le souhaitez, prenez encor ma vie;
> Pourvu que par ma mort tout le peuple irrité
> Ne vous ravisse pas ce qui m'a tant coûté.
>
> IV, 2

It is true that the ruthless, ambitious woman whose only purpose in life has been for years the conquest of power cannot without a fight resign herself to being only the subject of her son; she threatens him with a rival; she publicly declares that she will have Britannicus proclaimed by the praetorians; whether she realizes it or not she plots the death of her son. But, when the conspiracy shows sign of succeeding, when a powerful opposition groups itself around the pretender, when

> La moitié du Sénat s'intéresse pour nous:
> Sylla, Pison, Plautus . . .
>   (. . .) les chefs de la noblesse (. . .)
>
> III, 6

she has an instinctive recoil, and backs out. She cannot abandon
the supreme power she has wielded for so long, and she cannot
deliberately cause the downfall and the death of the son she
loves in her own imperious, jealous way.

Perhaps we are beginning to see the nature of Racinian
tragedy: it is the tragedy of the impossible choice, the tragedy
of the *impasse*. Britannicus must fight a battle he cannot win;
Néron will pay with his own life for the inevitable murder;
Agrippine must choose between murdering her own son and
being, eventually, murdered by him. For Néron, as well as for
Agrippine and Britannicus, it is impossible to reign without
crime; they must, as Pyrrhus harshly put it to Andromaque,
'ou périr ou régner'. For them, it seems, life itself is incompatible with innocence: the crime of Racine's heroes is to live.

In a less sombre manner, perhaps with some dubious rays of
hope, the nature of the tragic vision in *Andromaque* is the same;
it is also the tragedy of the *impasse* and the impossible choice.
Impasse of Andromaque, who cannot betray Hector, her husband, but who cannot sacrifice Astyanax, who is more than her
son and the son of Hector, who *is* Hector. *Impasse* of Hermione
who cannot accept that Pyrrhus should live unfaithful, or that
he should die even faithless:

> Ah! ne puis-je savoir si j'aime, ou si je hais!
>
> *Andr*. V, 1

As for Oreste, whether he is successful or not in his embassy,
whether Pyrrhus gives him the child he is demanding, or refuses
him, he will lose Hermione, who is all he cares for: for whether
he accepts to kill Pyrrhus, as she bids him to do, or refuses to
become a murderer for her sake, the result will be the same:
Pyrrhus will die, if not by his hand, by hers, and Hermione will
not survive him. Pyrrhus' choice is less stark; in marrying
Hermione, he might have lived and escaped Oreste's dagger,

but he would have denied not only his love but himself; in
choosing Andromaque, he denies his father, his country, and
his own past, and he chooses death, even if he does not know
it; but out of his death something perhaps will be born. The
ending of *Britannicus* is much darker; it is the end of the beginning, the curtain-raiser for the long career of crimes of Néron.

The *reconnaissance*

The tragic moment *par excellence* is the one of the *reconnaissance* (E. Vinaver), which is not the banal and somewhat
melodramatic recognition of the hidden or unknown identity
of one of the characters, but the moment when, in a kind of
sudden illumination, the character becomes fully aware of
something he always knew, but the full horror of which he had
never completely realized; it is the moment in which he has for
the first time a clear vision of the trap into which he has fallen,
of the *impasse* into which he has been driven. When Pyrrhus
has clearly stated to Andromaque the cruel bargain he is
striking with her:

> Songez-y: je vous laisse; et je viendrai vous prendre
> Pour vous mener au temple, où ce fils doit m'attendre,
> Et là vous me verrez, soumis ou furieux,
> Le couronner, Madame, ou le perdre à vos yeux.
>
> III, 7

Andromaque instinctively shrinks back:

> Non, je ne serai point complice de ses crimes.

But when her faithful confidant impatiently exclaims:

> Hé bien! allons donc voir expirer votre fils:
> On n'attend plus que vous.

then the full meaning of her action suddenly appears to Andromaque with blinding clarity:

> Ah! de quel souvenir viens-tu frapper mon âme!
> Quoi! Céphise, j'irai voir expirer encor
> Ce fils, (. . .)
>
> III, 8

When Hermione, torn between love and hatred, distractedly

wanders through Pyrrhus' palace, and finally opts for his death:

> Qu'il meure, puisqu'enfin il a dû le prévoir,
> Et puisqu'il m'a forcée enfin à le vouloir.

she listens with amazement and horror to her own condemnation:

> A le vouloir? Hé quoi? c'est donc moi qui l'ordonne?
> Sa mort sera l'effet de l'amour d'Hermione?
> Ce prince, dont mon cœur se faisait autrefois
> Avec tant de plaisir redire les exploits,
> A qui même en secret je m'étais destinée
> Avant qu'on eût conclu ce fatal hyménée,
> Je n'ai donc traversé tant de mers, tant d'Etats,
> Que pour venir si loin préparer son trépas?
>
> V, 1

Agrippine's first *reconnaissance* is more muted; she suddenly realizes that the conspirators are in earnest, that what she has willed is now coming into existence, that her son's life really is in danger – and that at the same time she cannot destroy him:

> Prince, que dites-vous?
> Sylla, Pison, Plautus! les chefs de la noblesse!
>
> *Brit*. III, 6

Her full illumination will come later, when the veil has been torn, and the new Néron stares her in the face:

> Ta main a commencé dans le sang de ton frère;
> Je prévois que tes coups viendront jusqu'à ta mère.
> Dans le fond de ton cœur je sais que tu me hais.
>
> V, 6

To Titus' dismissal Bérénice first reacts with an outburst of queenly pride:

> Moi-même j'ai voulu vous entendre en ce lieu.
> Je n'écoute plus rien; et pour jamais, adieu.

But this very word opens wide vistas of desolation which Bérénice only now realizes:

> Pour jamais! Ah! Seigneur, songez-vous en vous-même
> Combien ce mot cruel est affreux quand on aime?

Dans un mois, dans un an, comment souffrirons-nous,
Seigneur, que tant de mers me séparent de vous?
Que le jour recommence et que le jour finisse,
Sans que jamais Titus puisse voir Bérénice, (. . .)

Bér. IV, 5

The tragedy of self-destruction

It is a commonplace to remark that in seventeenth-century
French tragedy the action takes place in the hearts and minds
of the characters, but it is particularly true of the tragic action,
for the irony of Racinian tragedy is that his heroes are themselves the cause of their downfall. It is the arrival of Oreste
which precipitates the action, and is the immediate cause of
that which Oreste wanted most to avoid:

Le coup qui l'a perdu n'est parti que de lui.

Andr. III, 3

It is because Junie cannot bear the idea of Britannicus' misery
and despair that she escapes to reassure him, thus causing the
violent clash of the two rivals, which is followed by the arrest
of Britannicus. When Junie has at last guessed the depth of
Néron's hatred and hypocrisy, and vainly tries to prevent her
lover from going to the fateful banquet, it is Agrippine who
comes to hasten him to his death, and thus deprives herself of
her only weapon against Néron. It is Atalide's reproaches
which, in upsetting Bajazet, alert Roxane; it is her moment of
weakness that gives the Sultana the opportunity of seizing the
revealing letter. It is Mithridate who, by his unworthy ruses,
humiliates and angers Monime, and makes their marriage impossible. Consciously or unconsciously the Racinian hero
always seems to say the very words, to make the very gestures
that will deprive him of what he most desires, as if some power
in himself, some 'pensée imperceptible', as the Jansenist Nicole
put it, was at work to frustrate and to ruin him. And that perhaps appears most clearly in *Bérénice*.

The dislike of Rome for the alien Queen no doubt exists. The
risk of an insulting mob is not imaginary. The possibility of
disorders, of rioting which would have to be put down at the

cost of Roman blood cannot be excluded. The scruples of the new Emperor are honourable and sincere. But when all is said, the facts remain that the dangers are slight and remote, that the 'law' Titus invokes is irrational and crude, that it is in his power to ignore it, that Bérénice has made him what he is, and that he has a debt to her. Unless we say brutally that Titus has no love for Bérénice – which is a way to say that Racine did not know what play he was writing – what other solution is there except that Titus seeks not so much the accomplishment of a duty as the sacrifice and suffering that will come to him from denying himself what he most cherishes? Who, Bérénice asks, can prevent their happiness, when his father, who opposed the marriage, is dead, when Titus is all-powerful,

> Lorsque Rome se tait, quand votre père expire,
> Lorsque tout l'univers fléchit à vos genoux,
> Enfin quand je n'ai plus à redouter que vous?

Who indeed, but Titus, as he himself confesses it:

> Et c'est moi seul aussi qui pouvais me détruire.
>
> IV, 5

This is not Roman devotion to duty; it is a revealing light thrown upon the self-destructive and masochistic conception of 'duty' which is at the bottom of Jansenism and other similar forms of puritanism, to which Racine, alas, was only too prone.

The new tragedy then, Racinian tragedy, is one that, if we disregard its purely formal features, cuts adrift from all, or almost all, seventeenth-century drama. Its true, although remote, antecedents are to be found in Greek tragedy, but Racine has transformed them out of all recognition. Its tragic vision is infinitely darker than that of Corneille's drama, darker even than that of its Greek models. *Britannicus* or *Bérénice* need no Gods and no Fate, for their heroes carry in themselves the seeds of their misfortune and the irresistible impulses towards their own destruction.

6

Escape from Tragedy?

New trends

Like Corneille's, if within narrower limits, Racine's art has
evolved. It is a significant coincidence that, whatever their
approach or their criterion, all critics seem to distinguish two
manners, or two periods in Racine's non-biblical plays: to the
first, obviously, belong *Andromaque*, *Britannicus*, *Bérénice*; to
the second *Mithridate*, *Iphigénie* – with *Phèdre* in a class of her
own. In between is *Bajazet*.

There is much in *Bajazet* that reminds us of the past, and
Mauron is right to find in it the same pattern as in *Andromaque*
and *Britannicus*: Bajazet is between two women, a domineering
one he does not love, and a gentler one he does, just as Pyrrhus
is between Hermione and Andromaque, or Néron between
Agrippine and Junie. Using R. Barthes's formula, we could
say that 'A (Roxane) has absolute power over B (Bajazet)',
and that 'A loves B who does not love her'. We also find
again the theme of the 'captive', a strangely recurrent one
in Racine, from Andromaque and Junie to Eriphile and
Aricie, and the Reason of State is stated in a similar if more
brutal way. Useful as such formulae may be, it is also important
to note the differences, and to see the poet's imagination at
work, otherwise we might be led to think that he always wrote
the same play. First, in *Bajazet*, we have so to speak *Andromaque* reversed: the man is the captive of the woman. Atalide
desperately tries to save Bajazet as Junie attempts to protect
Britannicus, but Atalide has not the generosity and understanding of Junie, who does not retaliate against Britannicus' elaborate insults, and it is her ill-timed outburst of jealousy, not her

compassion, that is the immediate cause of Bajazet's death.
Like Hermione, the Sultana orders the death of her lover, and
it seemed she could not survive him:

> (. . .) crois-tu (. . .)
> Que si je perds l'espoir de régner dans (ton coeur)
> D'une si douce erreur si longtemps possédée,
> Je puisse désormais souffrir une autre idée,
> Ni que je vive enfin, si je ne vis pour toi? (. . .)
> De toi dépend ma joie et ma félicité.
> De ma sanglante mort ta mort sera suivie.
>
> *Baj.* II, 1

But in fact she will die by the Sultan's order, not by her own
hand. She is, it seems, the most cruel of Racine's characters,
more monstrous indeed than Néron. And finally Bajazet is a
somewhat new type in Racine: he is as powerless and *agi* as
Oreste, but with a coolness and steadiness Oreste lacked. He
constantly stares death in the face, and he is in no way the
hypocritical coward some critics have made him, for here we
must part company with R. Barthes who sees in him a handsome
male who barters his beauty for his life:

> Bajazet est aimable. Il vit que son salut
> Dépendait de lui plaire, et bientôt il lui plut.
>
> I, 1

These words are spoken by Acomat, who does not know the
real situation, and Bajazet acts his part – only under strong
pressure – with such disdainful detachment that it can be said
that he only allows Roxane to believe what she wishes to believe.
When she finally offers him his life on condition that he would
come with her to watch the death of Atalide at the hands of the
muets, he rejects her with angry contempt.

In another way too *Bajazet* is different: Racine has taken his
subject not only from Turkish history – he was not the first –
but from an almost contemporary incident in Constantinople
(Mourad IV died in 1640), for which he apologized in his Preface, alleging the example of Aeschylus' *Persians*. Instead of
the conventional combination of French and Roman attire the

play was acted in Oriental costumes. There is therefore in *Bajazet*, at least potentially, a fair amount of *couleur locale*, which, however, is not so much in visible picturesqueness as in the manners and institutions: sultans, viziers, janissaries, and *muets*; the constant atmosphere of terror which surrounds total despotism (in the very first scene the mere presence of Osmin, and even of Acomat in the harem would be, in normal times, punishable by death); the Sultans' practice, taken for granted, of having all their brothers strangled as soon as their rule is consolidated or they have an heir; the very existence of Amurat's awe-inspiring seraglio, citadel, palace, fortress, and prison, over which Roxane has absolute power:

> Et moi, vous le savez, je tiens sous ma puissance
> Cette foule de chefs, d'esclaves, de muets,
> Peuple que dans ces murs renferme ce palais,
> Et dont à ma faveur les âmes asservies
> M'ont vendu dès longtemps leur silence et leurs vies.
>
> II, 1

all this, with the fanatical mob and its leaders, the 'interpreters of the Faith', makes up quite a vivid tableau of a remote, half barbaric civilization. *Bajazet* suggests a tentative effort towards the later, spectacular drama of *Athalie*.

A tragedy of contingency

There is also in the play the number and importance of incidents; nothing 'happens' in *Bérénice*, many things do in *Bajazet*. At the start a messenger has come from Baghdad, where the Sultan prepares to fight a decisive battle: if he wins, his throne is secure; if he loses, his discontented troops will rise against him. But the road is long from Baghdad to Constantinople, and the issue has in fact already been decided: a second messenger, the sinister Orcan, brings the news of victory, as well as a second, more imperious order to have Bajazet executed. The already suspicious Roxane uses it to test Atalide who faints in dismay, which allows Roxane to take from her the damning letter written by Bajazet. But the Grand Vizier now plays his last desperate gamble: at the head of his armed friends he

breaks down the gates of the seraglio, and rushes to the rescue of
Bajazet . . . *Coup de théâtre*: Roxane is dead, stabbed by Orcan:

> Juste Ciel! l'innocence a trouvé ton appui.
>
> V, 10

exclaims Atalide. But Acomat was too late: Bajazet, after
fiercely defending himself, has been overpowered by the
muets . . . It is clear that *Bérénice* is not the only type of
Racinian tragedy. Roxane's deception, the lovers' misunderstanding, Atalide's fainting fit, the lost letter, the belated rescue,
too late by a few minutes, the false report, the *coup de théâtre*
. . . These things happen, but might not have happened. *If*
Acomat had known of Atalide's love . . . *if* he had attacked a
few minutes earlier . . . All these are accidents, contingent
events: the heroes fail, but they could have succeeded, their
dilemma is not insoluble, they are not caught in a dead-end.
This is one reason why *Bajazet* has been less admired, and
appears less tragic.

Another one is that the characters arouse less interest.
Bajazet is no coward, but it is true that during most of the play
he is impotent, and his stoic indifference, almost a bored
fatalism, does not stir us as do Oreste, Pyrrhus, Néron. The
main source of emotion seems to spring from Atalide, who, like
so many other Racinian characters, is the main cause of her
misfortune, and dies in bitterness and despair. But there is in
Atalide something feverish and unstable, a weakness, not in the
conception of the character, but in its moral fibre, and the
powerful figure of Roxane dominates the play to such an extent
that she throws all others into the shade. But can we, especially
at a time when we still hope for the sake of Bajazet, receive the
news of her death with anything but relief?

These doubts, however, may arise from too systematic a view
of tragedy and too simple a notion of the characters. In defence
of *Bajazet* it could be said that, when his life is at stake, man's
battle against the utter unpredictability of chance, this sinister
game of blindman's-buff which is part of man's condition, is a
kind of tragedy. More important, it could be said that *Bajazet*

is first of all 'the tragedy of Roxane' (J. Brody). In *Britannicus* the very ferocity of the protagonists, Néron and Agrippine, has often blinded the critics to the complex, even pathetic reality of their personal drama. With Roxane, even a Roxane who is more cruel and more implacable than Agrippine or Néron, we must not make the same mistake. The tragedy in *Bajazet* is as much in the ruin of Atalide and Bajazet as in the desperate efforts of Roxane not to see the fact of Bajazet's indifference, and in her final, tragic disillusion and *reconnaissance*. The three of them are re-united in all-levelling death, but Roxane's ordeal may not have been the lesser one.

Mithridate (1673)

We are now in the ancient East, in the days of Rome. But the East does not change much, and the world of *Mithridate* does not differ greatly from the world of *Bajazet*. At the beginning of the play, Mithridate, Rome's most formidable foe since Hannibal, seems at long last to have been destroyed: surprised in disarray by the Roman legions, his troops routed and dispersed, he has died an obscure, inglorious death. His two sons, Pharnace and Xipharès, are already quarrelling over his spoils: his kingdoms, and his Greek bride, the beautiful Monime, whom the King, after brutally trying to make her his concubine, had promised to make his Queen. Against Pharnace Monime already has begged Xipharès for help – when the sudden return of the King stops the guilty brothers. The crafty old despot had himself spread the false report, and his formidable presence at once silences his too hasty heirs. But he has seen through them; Pharnace first, who has sold out to Rome, is thrown into gaol. As for Xipharès, the wily Mithridate manages, by falsely pretending to give him Monime, to extract from her the secret of their love, and the King is preparing his revenge, when a second *coup de théâtre* shatters his plans: the Romans are attacking; they are at the gates of the palace; Pharnace has broken out of his prison and joined them; Xipharès is helping them. The old King at bay fights his last battle. Almost overwhelmed, he sends Monime the order to kill herself, and, not

to fall into the hands of Rome alive, he thrusts his sword into
his body . . . And that seems to be the expected *dénouement* to
a Racinian tragedy. But Mithridate has time to rescind his
order; Xipharès was not betraying the father he loves; he it is
who snatches victory from defeat and puts the mighty legions
to flight. Mithridate's last battle ends in triumph,

> Et (ses) derniers regards ont vu fuir les Romains.
>
> *Mithr.* V, 5

As a final reward the dying King gives his son his most priceless
possession: his bride.

> A mon fils Xipharès je dois cette fortune:
> Il épargne à ma mort leur présence importune.
> Que ne puis-je payer ce service important
> De tout ce que mon trône eut de plus éclatant!
> Mais vous me tenez lieu d'Empire, de couronne;
> Vous seule me restez: souffrez que je vous donne,
> Madame; (. . .)
>
> V, 6

Monime and Xipharès in tears beg him to live, but his only
concern is for the imminent clash with Rome, and his last words
are an order:

> Bientôt tous les Romains de leur honte irrités,
> Viendront ici sur vous fondre de tous côtés.
> Ne perdez point le temps que vous laisse leur fuite
> A rendre à mon tombeau des soins que je vous quitte.
> Tant de Romains sans vie, en cent lieux dispersés
> Suffisent à ma cendre et l'honorent assez.
> Cachez-leur pour un temps vos noms et votre vie.
> Allez, réservez-vous . . .
>   – Moi, Seigneur, que je fuie!
> Que Pharnace impuni, les Romains triomphants
> N'éprouvent pas bientôt . . .
>   – Non, je vous le défends. (. . .)

Xipharès will take up the struggle; Mithridate will survive himself in his son and in his glory. The cruel, suspicious tyrant dies
in an apotheosis. Grieved as they are, the blameless young
lovers are free. Admiration, compassion, relief leave the spectator moved and happy . . .

Tragedy, no doubt, is present in the play. It is in the desperate struggle of Mithridate against the invincible power of Rome, and in the onslaught of age, a more insidious, more implacable enemy. It is in his love, which gives him no happiness:

> Ce cœur nourri de sang, et de guerre affamé,
> Malgré le faix des ans et du sort qui m'opprime,
> Traîne partout l'amour qui l'attache à Monime.
>
> II, 3

a curse, and a poison:

> J'ai su, par une longue et pénible industrie,
> Des plus mortels venins prévenir la furie.
> Ah! qu'il eût mieux valu, plus sage et plus heureux,
> Et repoussant les traits d'un amour dangereux,
> Ne pas laisser remplir d'ardeurs empoisonnées
> Un cœur déjà glacé par le froid des années!
>
> IV, 5

It is above all in the self-destructive forces at work in Mithridate: his cruelty, which drives Pharnace to revolt and treason; his suspiciousness: he trusts no one, not even Xipharès and Monime, who were loyal to him. Monime will not forgive the cunning stratagem he resorts to to peer into the deepest recesses of her heart, and steal her secret. Mithridate himself has destroyed his most cherished desire. All the same there is little doubt that we are now at a considerable distance from the earlier plays. With its surprises and *coups de théâtre* the action is even more dramatic than in *Bajazet*. Chance also plays its part, but it now is the salvation of Xipharès and Monime, while it was the downfall of Atalide and Bajazet. For them there *is* a way out of the *impasse*; the trap does not close over its victims. However great the figure of Mithridate, however pathetic his fall, it brings a sense of relief, and, since *Alexandre*, this is the first of Racine's tragedies that ends in this way.

The appearance of the Father

Not only is the nature of the *dénouement* new: the character of Mithridate himself is without a precedent in his theatre. In *Andromaque*, from his distant Sparta, an angry Menelaus sends his daughter Hermione vain orders to return. In *Britannicus*, the murdered Claudius is safely dead and buried in the past. Vespasian, for many years the main obstacle to Bérénice's happiness, has at last joined the Immortals. In *Mithridate*, a vengeful Claudius, or Vespasian, too soon consigned to oblivion, returns from the dead. Ch. Mauron, and after him R. Barthes, have underscored the full significance in Racine's tragedy of this first appearance of the Father.

It is not only for Racine the occasion – the only one – of portraying an aged lover (there are several in Corneille) using his rank, his power, and the pledge given to him by Monime's father, to compete against younger rivals. It is that his rivals are his own sons. Such a situation is in no way unthinkable, but it is not an ordinary occurrence, and it does not seem unwarranted to remember here that this is an archetypal situation: in psychoanalysis it is the basic element of the Oedipian complex, the jealous, possessive love of the son for his mother and his violent resentment of the father's presence; in anthropology it takes us back to the primitive human Horde, in which the older, stronger male claims exclusive possession of the females, until the younger sons unite against him, and kill him. In one case the conflict is buried in the unconscious; in the other it is lost in the mists of time. These are hypotheses, useful models which are not susceptible of direct verification, but which at the same time do account for the violent emotional charge of the relationships they concern. They were often dramatized in very ancient stories or myths, and it seems fitting that, even before Racine turned to Hellenic mythology, his tragedy should already take on a mythical character.

What is even more striking, and ominous for the further development of Racine's tragic vision is the way this conflict is presented and resolved. However we may admire his courage and tenacity, however we may pity his harrowing dilemma, this first great Father-figure in Racine's theatre is far more monstrous than Néron or Roxane. Two of his sons already he has put to death; Xipharès' mother, who rebelled against him for obscure reasons, he has had executed; Pharnace, who plotted against him with Rome, can hope for no better treatment; to the bride he loves he sends the order to die; Xipharès, who knows him well, has no illusion about his father's intentions towards himself . . . The dangerous, treacherous tyrant brings death and destruction to all around him, and we should not be surprised to see him hated and destroyed by his intended victims. But facing the tyrannical Father stands the innocent Son, not only loyal and faithful to the end, but ready and willing to leave to his father the bride he himself loved long before she met Mithridate, and who loves him. It is Monime who rebels, but Xipharès' feeling of guilt is strong enough for him to watch his father make all preparations for his own execution without making a gesture to save himself, happy, when everything seems lost, to throw himself body and soul into the struggle to save the King from humiliation and defeat, and finally to beg him to live, and reign over them all, Monime included. Voltaire, mocking in him the submissive lover, 'doux et discret', of the novels, amazingly does not see that Xipharès, however generous to his mistress, sets more store by Mithridate than by Monime, and that he is ready to sacrifice her as well as himself to the towering figure of the Father.

The Cornelian moment

But the Father's unconditional authority has always been the linchpin not only of the family in its old, traditional conception, not only of all authoritarian societies, but more precisely of the feudal, aristocratic society that has dominated European history from the Middle Ages, and even more particularly of the baroque society often pictured in Corneille. With the resurgence of – or should we say the regression to ? – an ancient order which Racinian tragedy at first seemed set to destroy, a whole system of values angrily dismissed from the previous plays now reappears. Blood and Race, the powerful sense of Clan and Family, its Honour and its *Gloire* are, at least with Xipharès, linked with the keeping of one's Word, and, as apparent in his last words, the duty of Revenge. All these feelings are magnified by the elevation of the characters' rank – a

legendary King, crowned with 'trente diadèmes', master of the
Eastern Seas, a worthy enemy of Rome, instead of feudal lords,
or Roman patricians, but the values acknowledged in *Mithridate* are those we have become familiar with in *Le Cid*, *Horace*,
or *La Mort de Pompée*. This restoration of ancient values, to
which Hermione or Bérénice remained indifferent, is even more
striking in Monime. Promised to Mithridate by her father,
whose death at the hands of the Romans she wishes to avenge
by making common cause with the King, she only confesses her
love for Xipharès when she believes Mithridate to be dead (but
how quickly they are all ready to believe it!). As soon as she is
undeceived, she begs Xipharès never to see her again: her
gloire demands it, she has given her word. Xipharès can show
that he was worthy of her, that he *merited* her, only by
renouncing her for ever, and Xipharès bows at once to his
mistress' wish. It is the very situation of Pauline and Sévère in
Polyeucte; it is the Cornelian moment in Racine's play.

Ambivalence of *Mithridate*

Thus the appearance of the Father and the assertion of his
full authority have been enough to re-introduce into Racine's
tragedy a whole set of beliefs, traditions, and binding values,
which it had, it seemed, left behind. The presence of these
values – age-old, proven values, accepted by generations –
would be sufficient to change the nature of the *dénouement*:
even if the main characters perished as in *Andromaque* or
Bajazet, their death would have an objective sense, derived
from those universal values, whereas the heroes in *Andromaque*
or *Britannicus* deny all established values or create their own.
But in fact those characters we particularly wish to escape their
fate do survive; we mourn the passing away of a great ruler, but
we secretly sigh with relief that he could not achieve his murderous designs. This partly gives the play its ambivalence: its
tragic ending is a happy ending; it brings deliverance, not
catharsis. And, all along, the innocent Son proclaims his guilt,
and justifies the tyrannical Father, whose appalling cruelty
Racine has not been able, or willing, to conceal or condone. In

Xipharès and Monime it is all of Racine's great rebels that are denied, Jocaste, Pyrrhus, Oreste, Hermione, Roxane, Bérénice – although perhaps the seeds of Xipharès are already discernible in Titus' 'duty', infallibly recognizable as such because it demands the total sacrifice of self. It is Pharnace, not Xipharès, who is the true descendant of Pyrrhus. Yet Pharnace, a traitor to his country, his father, and his King, a deserter and a renegade, a brutal and a conceited lover, appears in a very unfavourable light by the side of his loyal, chivalrous brother; his final, ignominious flight with the Romans will not save him, as Mithridate prophesies, but his death will appear as just retribution. At the end, while the dutiful Son is preserved, the cruel Father is brought down, yet Racine strives to extol him, and all the values he stands for. Racine is still a rebel, but a rebel with a guilty, divided conscience.

Iphigénie (1674)

Much of what has been said of *Mithridate* could be said again of *Iphigénie*, which also has much that is strikingly new. The action is as dramatic, the surprises and *coups de théâtre* as well contrived as in *Mithridate*; indeed the character of Eriphile and the mystery of her birth seem at first sight to have been borrowed from the romances of the time. But for the first time since *La Thébaïde* and *Andromaque* Racine goes back to an old Greek legend, and whereas *La Thébaïde* was largely borrowed from Rotrou's *Antigone*, and in *Andromaque* Racine used reminiscences from Virgil, Homer, and Euripides, he now takes as his direct source a Greek tragedy, Euripides' *Iphigeneia in Aulis* (405 B.C.), and follows it closely. His own *Iphigénie* is a more polished play, more complex in its plot and its psychology, but it has perhaps not equalled the poignant greatness of its model. For the first time too since *La Thébaïde* the supernatural appears in Racine's theatre: with *Iphigénie* we enter the realm of legend, and the Gods are actively present in the play. Their intervention sets the drama in motion: a mysterious force has kept the Greek armada in Aulis just as it was setting sail for Troy. The wind has died away; the oarsmen's efforts are of no avail:

Nous partions; et déjà par mille cris de joie
Nous menacions de loin les rivages de Troie.
Un prodige étonnant fit taire ce transport:
Le vent qui nous flattait nous laissa dans le port.
Il fallut s'arrêter, et la rame inutile
Fatigua vainement une mer immobile.

Iph. I, 1

A miracle has occurred: as in Euripides the Goddess Artemis, or Diane, as Racine calls her, will not allow the ships to sail. Her anger – left in Racine quite unexplained – demands a human sacrifice, the sacrifice of Iphigénie. So said the oracle, as read by the High Priest, Calchas, who has so far kept it a secret from the Army, but who could at any moment let loose its fanatical passions. Calchas, who never appears on the stage, is the real master of the situation. He is as formidable as the unseen Amurat in *Bajazet*. Ulysse, the Machiavellian figure in the play, is aware of it, and advises circumspection. Agamemnon is afraid of him. His prophetic gift will be given the seal of authenticity when a second miracle closes the tragedy: as soon as the blood of the victim has been shed,

Les Dieux font sur l'autel entendre le tonnerre,
Les vents agitent l'air d'heureux frémissements,
Et la mer leur répond par ses mugissements.
La rive au loin gémit, blanchissante d'écume,
La flamme du bûcher d'elle-même s'allume.

V, 6

Like *Mithridate*, in an even more marked way, *Iphigénie* is a tragedy of war, and its virtues are the war-like virtues of a military caste, courage and self-sacrifice; its values are those of an authoritarian, aristocratic society: the mystic value of Blood and Race; the absolute power of the father over his children, and the absolute obedience of the children to the father; and above all, *gloire*, which is, more narrowly perhaps than in Corneille, the need to preserve one's reputation with one's peers, and even more to inspire the soldiers with the proper kind of admiration and awe for their betters. The Army, the People, the Crowd, never absent from Racine's tragedies, here play a more insistent part than in any other one, and their irrational lust to conquer and to loot has now the sanction of Religion. From the start the spiritual climate of *Iphigénie* is far removed from that of *Andromaque*, *Britannicus*, or *Bérénice*.

The King of Kings

Gloire seems indeed the *leitmotiv* of the tragedy. Agamemnon's *gloire*: his first appearance is a truly majestic one. He is a divine King, descended from the Gods, the richest and the most powerful of the Greek sovereigns who have elected him as their leader, the King of Kings, and the harmonious, elegiac lines in which he meditates over the vanity of all grandeurs seem to crown him with a halo of noble melancholy:

> Heureux qui satisfait de son humble fortune,
> Libre du joug superbe où je suis attaché,
> Vit dans l'état obscur où les Dieux l'ont caché!

I, 1

But precisely kingship, to Agamemnon, is mainly a burden:

> Triste destin des rois! Esclaves que nous sommes
> Et des rigueurs du sort, et des discours des hommes!
> Nous nous voyons sans cesse assiégés de témoins;
> Et les plus malheureux osent pleurer le moins!

I, 5

And it is a burden he seems unable to accept, or to lay down. *Iphigénie* is, or seems at first to be, the tragedy of a man who cannot make up his mind. And if the *gloire* of the hero consists – as it does in Corneille – to surmount his most legitimate desires and his dearest wishes, Agamemnon is no hero. When he was first told of the oracle demanding his daughter's life, he refused pointblank. But, Ulysse says, his *gloire* demands it, for if he demurs, after marshalling such a mighty host, he will be an object of derision. What is *gloire* in this context but the fear of opinion:

> Roi sans gloire, j'irais vieillir dans ma famille!

and the pleasurable contemplation of his glittering titles:

Charmé de mon pouvoir, et plein de ma grandeur,
Ces noms de roi des rois et de chef de la Grèce
Chatouillaient de mon cœur l'orgueilleuse faiblesse

I, 1

But after all, what seems weakness perhaps is duty? At the beginning of a costly war in which so many brave men are ready
to lay down their lives for the honour of Greece, will he give up
everything, Ulysse says, 'pour un peu de sang'? Agamemnon
has yielded:

De ma fille, en pleurant, j'ordonnai le supplice.

I, 1

But when the play begins, in the middle of the night, Agamemnon has changed his mind: his past decision fills him with
horror. In haste he sends a messenger to stop his daughter's
progress towards Aulis. Alas! in the darkness the messenger
misses the royal procession: Iphigénie and her mother make
their entry into the camp. Agamemnon resigns himself to the
inevitable. For three acts he will lie and scheme to deceive his
formidable Queen, Clytemnestre, and his daughter herself, who
is preparing to go to the altar to marry Achille, when she is
told, in the most striking *coup de théâtre* so far devised by
Racine, that the wedding altar is to be a sacrificial one. Agamemnon holds on against the touching prayers of his daughter,
against the threats and curses of his wife, against the wrath of
Achilles, but suddenly, unable to bear it any more, he hastily
contrives Iphigénie's escape, which ends in failure. After which
the King of Kings fades out of the action: the last image of him
is at the altar, veiling his face . . . refusing to see what he has
all the time willed and unwilled, steady only in irresolution. A
fascinating study in deviousness and self-contradiction, but an
unheroic figure; a tender-hearted father no doubt, as in Euripides, subtly combined by Racine with the inefficient general,
the inept, arrogant leader of the *Iliad*. His *gloire* has indeed
been thrust upon him, not conquered; it is the *gloire* of his high
office, or, as Pascal would say, a *grandeur d'établissement*.

Triumph of the hero

Turning away from the treacherous, murderous Father, we
are on firmer ground with the couple of fiancés, Achille and
Iphigénie. Achille is an entirely new type in Racine, the irre-
pressible, unconquerable, and finally triumphant hero, and it
seems pointless to complain that he does not find, to express
his love, the accents of Pyrrhus, Oreste, or Hippolyte; his love
he expresses in his acts. With Achille Racine abandons Euripides. The Euripidean Achilles is the prodigious athlete, 'swift
Achilles', running level with a chariot drawn by four horses at
full gallop; but he is also, unexpectedly, a bashful adolescent,
overwhelmed by the unusual situation in which he finds himself. He is not in love with Iphigeneia, whom he has never seen
before, but her heroic acceptance and tragic solitude move him
to compassion and admiration, and he offers to protect her as
her husband. When she refuses he bows to her will, and solemn-
ly performs his part in the ritual of the sacrifice. The Racinian
Achille is Homer's Achilles, and through him, rare achievement, we reach towards the epic and tragic greatness of the
ancient poet. Achille, son of a goddess, has been given the
choice between a quiet, obscure existence in his native Thessaly,
and a brief, splendid life, with a fame that will resound through
the centuries; he has chosen greatness, and will pay the price.
Achille does not deny the Gods: he constantly strives to be one:

> L'honneur parle, il suffit: ce sont là nos oracles.
> Les Dieux sont de nos jours les maîtres souverains;
> Mais, Seigneur, notre gloire est dans nos propres mains.
> Pourquoi nous tourmenter de leurs ordres suprêmes?
> Ne songeons qu'à nous rendre immortels comme eux-
>   mêmes.

> I, 2

The King of Kings he despises, as a leader and as a father; he
insults him to his face, in an outburst of princely arrogance
which preserves something from the tremendous power of his
remote, Homeric model; and Agamemnon's unnatural behaviour to his daughter has robbed him in his eyes of the mystic

halo of the father; to him the father is, in R. Barthes's words, entirely 'désacralisé'. He alone dares to defy Calchas, and the Gods themselves, and to Clytemnestre he promises her daughter's life:

> (. . .) croyez que tant que je respire,
> Les Dieux auront en vain ordonné son trépas:
> Cet oracle est plus sûr que celui de Calchas.

> III, 7

While Agamemnon veils his face Achille draws up the small band of his own warriors around Iphigénie, and prepares to defend her against the whole Greek army. And who knows if Calchas' sudden illumination has not something to do with this determined stand? . . . One is at a loss to understand how generations of critics could dismiss such a powerful creation as an insipid fop, or a French courtier.

A Racinian heroine

In Iphigénie are embodied all the values which the play magnifies: the heroic submission to the father's authority; when Agamemnon's lies are laid bare, she at once reassures him:

> Mon père,
> Cessez de vous troubler, vous n'êtes point trahi.
> Quand vous commanderez, vous serez obéi.
> Ma vie est votre bien. (. . .)
> D'un œil aussi content, d'un cœur aussi soumis
> Que j'acceptais l'époux que vous m'aviez promis,
> Je saurai, s'il le faut, victime obéissante,
> Tendre au fer de Calchas une tête innocente.

> IV, 4

Pride in her race and exalted rank:

> Ne craignez rien. Mon cœur, de votre honneur jaloux,
> Ne fera pas rougir un père tel que vous.

> IV, 4

The calm acceptance of death in the middle of tears and confusion:

> D'un peuple impatient vous entendez la voix.

she tells her mother:

Daignez m'ouvrir vos bras pour la dernière fois,
Madame, et rappelant votre vertu sublime . . .
Eurybate, à l'autel conduisez la victime.

V, 3

No Cornelian heroine ever went further. Yet Iphigénie has
unmistakably the stamp of Racine. She loves Achille, and her
love, for all her admiration and pride in her young hero, is the
exclusive, jealous love of a Racinian heroine. When it seems
she has a rival, Iphigénie suddenly reveals that she is after all of
the blood of Helen and Hermione. In a flash she sees through
Eriphile, and devines her repressed, tortured love for the brutal
warrior who has snatched her from her native Lesbos, in the
middle of the looting and slaughtering in the blazing town:

> Oui, vous l'aimez, perfide.
> Et ces mêmes fureurs que vous me dépeignez,
> Ces bras que dans le sang vous avez vus baignés,
> Ces morts, cette Lesbos, ces cendres, cette flamme,
> Sont les traits dont l'amour l'a gravé dans votre âme;
> Et loin d'en détester le cruel souvenir,
> Vous vous plaisez encore à m'en entretenir.

II, 5

This is no sweet, innocent child, but a woman wounded in her
love and her pride. And when Iphigénie accepts a death that
appears imminent there is, mixed with self-sacrifice, despair:
Agamemnon, angered by Achille's threats and defiance, has
sworn that even if he succeeds in saving his daughter she will
never belong to Achille, and life now appears to Iphigénie
empty. Yet she finds solace in the thought that it is thanks to
her that Achille will conquer fame and greatness:

> Songez, Seigneur, songez à ces moissons de gloire
> Qu'à vos vaillantes mains présente la victoire. (. . .)
> Si je n'ai pas vécu la compagne d'Achille,
> J'espère que du moins un heureux avenir
> A vos faits immortels joindra mon souvenir;
> Et qu'un jour mon trépas, source de votre gloire,
> Ouvrira le récit d'une si belle histoire.

V, 2

Escape from tragedy?

A father torn between his duty as a King – or is it his ambition? or his weakness? – and his love for a daughter he finally
sentences to death; a noble heroine accepting to die for her
father, her lover, and her country; a rebel to the priests, the
soldiers, and the kings, ready to defend her against all, even
against the Gods – cruel, enigmatic Gods, who demand a
human sacrifice and an innocent victim, this is indeed a pathetic,
and a tragic situation, but . . . But it was all a misunderstanding. 'How could I,' Racine writes in his Preface, 'defile the
stage with the horrifying murder of so virtuous and so
lovable a character as Iphigénie had to appear?' We learn, not
without amazement, from the author of *Britannicus*, and later
of *Phèdre*, that virtue, beauty, and charm make a person im-
mune from the blows of Fate. We thought that he had learned
from the Greeks that they drew the angry *nemesis* of the jealous
Gods. Agamemnon and Clytemnestre will soon embrace their
daughter; Achille and the King will be reconciled; Clytemnestre gratefully thanks Achille and the Gods, no longer the
cruel, enigmatic Gods, but a Providence, a supreme Power that
always means the greatest good in all it does, a Power that in
its mysterious way led all the characters to joy and happiness.
This is indeed escape from tragedy.

Not quite, however. The blood of a victim will flow. The
Gods will not be deprived of their expected feast. Another
Iphigénie – for such is the true identity of Eriphile – will be
sacrificed, the bastard child of an illegitimate union of Helen of
Troy and Theseus. This romantic invention leaves us somewhat
incredulous, yet it is worthy of a closer examination. It seems
that Racine has lost no opportunity of arousing antipathy towards this dark Iphigénie, who seems a negative replica, or
double, of her luminous sister. Her masochistic, morbid love for
the destroyer of her city, her hatred for Iphigénie who loved her,
her base betrayal of Agamemnon's last-minute effort to save his
daughter (it is Ériphile who rushes to warn Calchas so that a mob
of soldiers prevent Iphigénie's escape by force), her presence
at the altar when Iphigénie is on the point of death, while she

(. . .) peut-être en son cœur
Du fatal sacrifice accusait la lenteur,

V, 6

(or so says Ulysse), everything concurs to blacken Eriphile. In the midst of general relief, of reconciliation and rejoicing, when hymns of gratitude are raised to the providential Gods, who cares for Eriphile? let her die, and good riddance!

It cannot be said that Racine has not willed this reaction on the part of the spectators, or is not responsible for it; together with the dramatic impact and intense pathos of the play, the *dénouement* played a large part in making *Iphigénie* his most successful production. But a play in which, however poignant the situation, the characters we identify with finally escape their peril, a play in which the only victim arouses no sympathy and little compassion, such a play can be a masterpiece of a kind, but it is not tragic.

Eriphile's *noire destinée*

Even if *Iphigénie* is not a tragedy – by the strict standards of Aristotle, and of Racine himself – there is no doubt, however, that Eriphile's fate is a tragic one. She does not know herself, and like the ancient Oedipus, and as the oracle has predicted, she cannot know herself, and live. In a play in which high birth is a dominant theme, her bastardy can only arouse disdain, or at best compassion – which she gets from Iphigénie alone, and for which, expectedly perhaps, she is not grateful. Eriphile has never known a father or a mother, and she is made to pay for it every day of her life. There was here, it seems, grounds for sympathy; indeed we faintly discern the possible outlines of a sentimental, 'larmoyant', eighteenth-century type of heroine . . . which Racine has not allowed to emerge. What does emerge instead, is a painful, disquieting truth, which is that all that in Eriphile could have aroused sympathy, in fact goes into making her a destructive and a deadly character. But there is more to this than one of those illuminations of the depths of the psyche of which Racine offers not a few examples. For *Iphigénie*, with its Gods and Goddesses, its divine Kings, its miracles, oracles, and prophetic dreams is well on its way to becoming what *Phèdre* and *Athalie* will be, a sacred drama, and it is not so much a psychological mechanism that Racine suggests through Eriphile as a divine will. Like Oedipus, like his sons, the *frères ennemis* of *La Thébaïde*, Eriphile's first crime was to be born, for from her first hour she was fated to misfortune; Calchas was present at her birth:

> Je vis moi-même alors ce fruit de leurs amours.
> D'un sinistre avenir je menaçai ses jours.
> Sous un nom emprunté sa noire destinée
> Et ses propres fureurs ici l'ont amenée.
>
> V, 6

Is her *noire destinée* enough to account for, and perhaps to excuse, her *propres fureurs*? In the light of *Iphigénie* it appears not. The base, treacherous, ungrateful, murderous nature of Eriphile, abandoned by her creator himself to the hatred and contempt of all, has *justified* the Gods, and by her wicked deeds Eriphile herself has, after the event, so to speak, deserved and ratified their verdict, and made manifest their wisdom.

Indeed we do not have to be told that Eriphile is Racine's invention, and that she does not belong to the world of Greece. The Sophoclean *Oedipus* tells of the fall of a great King, who was just and compassionate, and whom the Gods destroyed. The Gods are our masters, but we can still grieve over their victim. This Racine does not allow, and it introduces into his tragedy a new, ominous element. An element that is foreign to Greek tragedy, for the cruelty of the Greek Gods has a cleaner edge, and their injustice is at the same time more patent and more mysterious. But also an element that was foreign to Racine's tragedy. For Eriphile could say to Heaven, as Oreste did:

> J'étais né pour servir d'exemple à ta colère.
>
> *Andr.* V, 5

But we could still pity Oreste fallen into the snare of the Gods; we could still side with him in spite of his faults and his crimes. Eriphile is the first of Racine's characters who is not only crushed by Fate but damned by men and Gods alike.

7

Phèdre

Myths, Gods, and demigods.

What is striking in *Phèdre*, compared not only with *Britannicus*
or *Bérénice* but with *Andromaque* or even *Iphigénie*, is the importance Racine has given to the mythical or legendary element.
The evocative names of ancient Greece, and the faint outlines of
its dark or luminous myths hover, as in a Mallarméan half-
dream, over its imagined landscape:

> J'ai couru les deux mers que sépare Corinthe;
> J'ai demandé Thésée aux peuples de ces bords
> Où l'on voit l'Achéron se perdre chez les morts;
> J'ai visité l'Elide, et laissant le Ténare,
> Passé jusqu'à la mer qui vit tomber Icare.
>
> *Ph.* I, 1

And the exploits of Thésée, the successor of Heracles, suggest
heroic battles against monstrous enemies of a still recent past:

> Les monstres étouffés et les brigands punis, (. . .)
> Et les os dispersés du géant d'Epidaure,
> Et la Crète fumant du sang du Minotaure.
>
> I, 1

But the evocation of the myths does more than create an atmosphere, or surround the hero with the halo of legend; it is
part of them, like the blood in their veins. Hippolyte, the youthful hero who fights back the surge of passion in himself,
who recoils in disgust from Phèdre's incestuous love, is the
son of Antiope, Queen of the war-like Amazons, the Wild
Women who despised love, Phèdre is descended from the Sun:

> Toi dont ma mère osait se vanter d'être fille, (. . .)
> Soleil, je te viens voir pour la dernière fois.
>
> I, 3

She is

> La fille de Minos et de Pasiphaé.
>
> I, 1

Minos dwells among the dead:

> Minos juge aux Enfers tous les pâles humains.
>
> IV, 6

And as for Pasiphaé, Racine has not shrunk from conjuring up her monstrous union with the White Bull of Crete. Phèdre is the daughter of lawless passion and severe conscience, poised between Life and Death, between Light and Darkness. And if Racine has achieved the *tour de force* of breathing life into the worn out images of ancient fables, it is because of the intensity with which they live in the minds and hearts of his heroes. Thésée has escaped from a long and harsh prison,

> (. . .) cavernes sombres,
> Lieux profonds et voisins de l'empire des ombres.
>
> III, 5

the very rhymes echoing the rumours whispered among the people of Trézène:

> On sème de sa mort d'incroyables discours. (. . .)
> On dit même, et ce bruit est partout répandu,
> Qu'avec Pirithoüs aux Enfers descendu,
> Il a vu le Cocyte et les rivages sombres,
> Et s'est montré vivant aux infernales ombres.
>
> II, 1

But what is to the sceptic Aricie, daughter of the Earth, no more than dubious hearsay, Phèdre, passionately, triumphantly, states as indisputable fact, and her very passion gives it reality:

> On ne voit point deux fois le rivage des morts,
> Seigneur. Puisque Thésée a vu les sombres bords,
> En vain vous espérez qu'un Dieu vous le renvoie,
> Et l'avare Achéron ne lâche point sa proie.
>
> II, 5

Thésée's most famous deed, the descent into the Labyrinth, and the killing of the Minotaur, takes up a new life in Phèdre's feverish imagination, in which Hippolyte assumes the place of Thésée.

> C'est moi, Prince, c'est moi dont l'utile secours
> Vous eût du Labyrinthe enseigné les détours.
> Que de soins m'eût coûtés cette tête charmante!
> Un fil n'eût point assez rassuré votre amante.
> Compagne du péril qu'il vous fallait chercher,
> Moi-même devant vous j'aurais voulu marcher;
> Et Phèdre au Labyrinthe avec vous descendue
> Se serait avec vous retrouvée, ou perdue.
>
> II, 5

This is no longer image or metaphor; it is an hallucinated projection of Phèdre's desire and maternal tenderness for 'cette tête charmante', as well as of her total gift of herself. And after Thésée's curse, after he has begged the God to destroy his son, we know that Hippolyte cannot escape:

> Misérable, tu cours à ta perte infaillible.
> Un Dieu vengeur te suit, tu ne peux l'éviter.
>
> III, 3

The final prodigy will not surprise us, and when, in his first and last battle, the young hero has defeated the dragon Neptune has sent against him, the Sea-God himself will appear, goading the bolting horses which will break his chariot to pieces, and smash their master against the rocks.

Orchestration of *Phèdre*

Phèdre (1677) is, like *Iphigénie*, derived from Euripides, whose *Hippolytos* (428 B.C.) has been Racine's main source, with Seneca a secondary one, but '*Phèdre* summarizes Racine's theatre' (Mauron), and all his dominant themes are to be found in it. From Euripides Racine has borrowed his three main characters: Thésée, the murderous Father – Hippolyte, the innocent Son – Phèdre, the incestuous Mother. In *Phèdre* the unfulfilled threat of Mithridate or Agamemnon is finally ac-

complished: Thésée does bring death upon his son, and if
Agrippine, the jealous, possessive mother, recoiled from killing
Néron, Phèdre's incestuous love bursts into the open, and she
will, in a trance of jealousy, almost absent-mindedly, let Hippolyte die (the incest being thinly disguised for the sake of
bienséances: Phèdre is Hippolyte's stepmother). The happiness
refused to the youthful couples of Junie and Britannicus, or
Bajazet and Atalide, is even more brutally denied to Hippolyte
and Aricie – a character of Racine's invention, who is indis-
pensable to the psychological economy of the play, and who
does not any more than Britannicus deserve to be ironically
shrugged off. Politics obviously do not play the same part in
Phèdre as in *Britannicus*, but they are far from absent: when, to
Hippolyte's naïve dismay, Phèdre's son is chosen as the successor of Thésée instead of the legitimate heir, Aricie, the crown of
Athens is the glittering prize which Phèdre tries to use to buy
Hippolyte's goodwill, and hopefully his love. Finally the social
values which were challenged in *Andromaque* and *Britannicus*
are again, as in *Mithridate* and *Iphigénie*, strongly asserted,
whether it be the absolute right of the father over his son, or of
the King over his subjects, the sacred character of marriage
and the family, the right of revenge against the defiler of Blood
and Race. But all those high-sounding names finally appear as
sheer mockery when the Father turns against his blameless Son
and sheds his own blood, when the august figure of the King is
carried away by blind rage, and condemns an innocent without
hearing him, when his Queen is an adulteress, when the dutiful
Son himself challenges the Father, when finally the Gods themselves appear unworthy of reverence. For through and beyond
its social, psychological implication and its poetic symbols,
Phèdre exists at the level of a sacred drama, and its characters
assume cosmic, metaphysical dimensions.

We have seen how carefully Racine wove the myths into the
texture of his play, and into the minds of his heroes. This is
partly what shocked and confused the contemporaries, who
complained that the play was unintelligible unless imaginary
figures such as Neptune and Venus were granted real existence

and power. It would of course be silly to ask if Racine 'believed' in Venus in the way in which Aphrodite and Poseidon were great and fearful deities to Aeschylus, Sophocles, or Euripides, but there is nothing extraordinary in a poet using myths as a coherent system of symbols to convey a genuine vision of life. We may of course re-interpret such 'realities' in modern, different terms, but we cannot without destroying the poetry or the meaning of the tragedy treat them as figures of speech or ornaments of style. This is true of Phèdre who, Racine says in his Preface, 'is led (. . .) by the wrath of the Gods into a passion which she is the first to abominate' and whose 'crime is rather a punishment inflicted by the Gods than an impulsion of her will'; and it also gives the character and the fate of Hippolyte their full meaning.

The tragedy of Hippolyte

Hippolyte has often been treated with scant regard, and it may be useful to clear the ground of much hostile criticism he has incurred. Schlegel bitterly reproached Racine for having trivialized him and replaced the strange beauty of Euripides' hero by French 'galanterie'. L. Goldmann sees him 'sans consistance réelle . . . le personnage qui fuit', whose virtue is nothing but 'pauvreté et faiblesse'. There is no doubt that Racine's Hippolyte is very far from Euripides': the Orphic initiate, the worshipper of Artemis, Goddess of virginity and wild life, and patroness of hunters, is irretrievably lost, and it could not be otherwise: Racine's poetry does not indulge in archaeology. Something, however, persists of him in Hippolyte's melancholy memory of a lost happiness: the joyful hunter in Racine is the Hyppolyte of the past; Théramène, his tutor, has noted that

> On vous voit moins souvent, orgueilleux et sauvage,
> Tantôt faire voler un char sur le rivage,
> Tantôt, savant dans l'art par Neptune inventé,
> Rendre docile au frein un coursier indompté.
> Les forêts moins souvent de nos cris retentissent.

I, 1

And Hippolyte will confess it:

> Mon arc, mes javelots, mon char, tout m'importune.
>
> II, 2

Another reproach made to Racine is that Hippolyte, when accused by Thésée of rape, keeps silent out of an absurd respect for the *bienséances*, losing his honour and his life for the sake of politeness – the French courtier again! – unable even to hint at the ugly truth. But one must be very hard of hearing to speak of Hippolyte's silence. He is no doubt stunned by the enormity of the accusation, but his first reaction is revealing: Phèdre, of all people, dares to accuse me! When he has recovered from his surprise he says it plainly: Phèdre is lying: 'un mensonge si noir'; Phèdre knows that he is speaking the truth:

> Phèdre au fond de son coeur me rend plus de justice.

And at last he accuses in his turn, and, in the most daring terms, reminds Thésée of Phèdre's tainted blood, and of the monstrous mating of Pasiphaé:

> Vous me parlez toujours d'inceste et d'adultère!
> Je me tais. Cependant Phèdre sort d'une mère,
> Phèdre est d'un sang, Seigneur, vous le savez trop bien,
> De toutes ces horreurs plus rempli que le mien.
>
> IV, 3

If he says no more it is because Thésée, literally mad with fury, threatens to have him thrown out of the palace by brute force.

Finally, if we missed in Achille the intensity of Oreste or Pyrrhus, it is unmistakably present in Hippolyte. Théramène has observed it:

> Chargés d'un feu secret, vos yeux s'appesantissent.
>
> I, 1

Hippolyte himself will express it in lines that are among the most suggestive and haunting of Racine's:

> Depuis près de six mois, honteux, désespéré,
> Portant partout le trait dont je suis déchiré,
> Contre vous, contre moi, vainement je m'éprouve:
> Présente, je vous fuis; absente, je vous trouve;
> Dans le fond des forêts votre image me suit; (. . .)

Moi-même, pour tout fruit de mes soins superflus,
Maintenant je me cherche, et ne me trouve plus.

II, 2

If we tried to psychoanalyse the poet through the poem we might of course say that Hippolyte with his guilty love is but a reflection and a double of Phèdre, but at the level of literary analysis and of the explicit meaning of the play, we have no right to say, as some did, that those lines 'really' belong to Phèdre.

For, however pervasive the presence of Phèdre, there is also, in the play – to say nothing of the tragedy of Thésée, and even of Aricie, or Œnone – the tragedy of Hippolyte. The tragedy of Hippolyte is not just that he dies a violent and cruel death. Or that he is cut down in the flower of his youth, at the very moment and on the very spot where he expected to meet Aricie and make her his wife. Not even that he measures himself against, and is destroyed by, the invincible power of Neptune. It is that he dies an innocent by the hand of a God. The tragedy of Hippolyte's death is the scandal of divine injustice.

Of course Racine, mindful of Aristotle's principle, that a tragic hero should not be totally evil or perfectly virtuous, has not presented Hippolyte as a model of bland innocence and guileless virtue. When he first appears and confesses his love it is with a strong feeling of guilt: Thésée has forbidden Aricie to marry, and there is logic if not justice in his defence. Aricie is the last survivor of the rival dynasty of the massacred Pallantides, and Thésée will not allow her to bring forth an heir and an avenger. Hippolyte is well aware he is disobeying his father's order on a vital matter. When he finally makes his choice he draws its full consequences, and having embraced Aricie's cause, he prepares for open war:

De puissants défenseurs prendront notre querelle;
Argos nous tend les bras, et Sparte nous appelle.

V, 1

There is nothing in Hippolyte of Xipharès' meekness. But the fact remains that he dies for a crime of which he is totally innocent. Against the prodigy, against the terrifying presence of the God, in the face of death, Hippolyte, to the very end protests his innocence:

Le Ciel, dit-il, m'arrache une innocente vie.

V, 6

This takes us a long way from *Iphigénie*, in which the Gods finally assumed the reassuring, traditional form of a Providence; a victim was sacrificed, it is true, but she aroused little sympathy. As for Iphigénie, Racine, he said, could not bring himself to show the death of 'so lovable and virtuous a person'. But Hippolyte is no less virtuous and lovable. The Gods who, maliciously or ironically, grant Thésée his murderous wish can lay no claim to any moral or providential character. There is no accounting for the manifestations of their will; Phèdre they never help, Hippolyte they kill, Thésée they protect, and their capricious protection turns out to be as deadly as their indifference. The Racinian world, which, in *Britannicus* or *Bérénice*, seemed to be empty of Gods, appears now to be ruled by incomprehensible Powers which are entirely dissociated from any moral purpose.

The tragedy of Phèdre

Phèdre's experience, however, far surpasses in tragic horror that of Hippolyte, and in fact anything Racine had so far imagined. The starting point – although not necessarily the conclusion – in our examination of Phèdre may well be Racine's own view of his heroine, as he expresses it in his Preface: she has, he says, all the characters which Aristotle requires from the tragic hero to arouse compassion and terror, for 'she is not altogether guilty, nor is she altogether innocent'. And, Racine, it seems wishes to insist on her innocence, since he reminds us that the primary cause of her passion is 'the wrath of the Gods', a 'punishment' (for what?) inflicted by them rather than 'an impulsion of her own will'. It would seem that, if Phèdre is the victim of an all-powerful deity, she can hardly be called guilty. Unless we decide that Venus is a mere metaphor, a 'poetic', or

allegorical, way of personifying her love, an 'embellishment'
such as Boileau conceived the use of mythology:

> Chaque vertu devient une divinité :
> Minerve est la prudence, et Vénus la beauté.
>
> *Art Poétique*, III, 165

Or unless we see Venus as a paltry excuse, and the form taken
by Phèdre's bad faith. Yet this runs counter to the whole play:
Venus lives in the body and the mind of Phèdre. To her she is a
real and constant presence; a malevolent will that has pur-
sued her family generation after generation; a sphinx holding
her in her claws, 'Vénus tout entière à sa proie attachée', not
an elegant allegory of 'Beauty'. To her Phèdre has built a
temple, to her she raises a mournful prayer that seems to echo
in advance the Baudelairian *Litanies de Satan*:

> O toi qui vois la honte où je suis descendue,
> Implacable Vénus, suis-je assez confondue ?
> Tu ne saurais plus loin pousser ta cruauté.
> Ton triomphe est parfait ; tous tes traits ont porté.
>
> III, 2

In which way then can she be guilty? It is difficult on this
point to follow R. Barthes, and to see her first fault in the confession Œnone forces out of her. Œnone is not a mere sound-
ing board, like so many confidants. Racine has given her a
background, a past, and a motivation. She is to Phèdre a more
earthly mother than the half-mythical Pasiphaé: the silence of
Phèdre drives her to despair, and almost to suicide, as Phèdre's
curse will finally do. A refusal here would be inhuman, and
in fact not credible. More serious the confession Phèdre makes
of her love to Hippolyte himself, for she has never accepted
Œnone's facile way out that the death of Thésée makes her
passion 'une flamme ordinaire'. But her confession was not pre-
meditated; she came for the sake of her son; the actual
presence of Hippolyte was too much for her:

> J'oublie, en le voyant, ce que je viens lui dire.
>
> II, 5

In one scene at least, however, Phèdre, lucidly, unreservedly, yields to her love. At the beginning of Act III she is no longer the exhausted, dying Phèdre of her first appearance; her mind is made up. The humiliation of a rebuff she accepts; the rights of her son, which she had gone to Hippolyte to defend, she abandons without a fight, if a royal crown may win her his love. She stubbornly argues with Œnone, who now tries to stop her. She finally commands her, and bullies her into a second approach to Hippolyte. And finally in her panic at Thésée's return she commits the unforgivable crime if not to speak against him, at least to allow Œnone to accuse him. Unforgivable it would be, that is, if almost at once Phèdre, terrified, did not go to her husband to save his son . . . But the news of Hippolyte's love for Aricie leaves her speechless with surprise. Here again Phèdre's crime is not in what she says, but in her silence. For a while Phèdre is transformed into an avenging Fury: she no longer cares for Hippolyte; she no longer bothers about the truth; she passionately desires Aricie's death, and let Thésée choose the cruellest one:

> Qu'il ne se borne pas à des peines légères!

Indeed Phèdre here is no longer innocent. But almost at once she rises above the storm and confusion of her passions, and the look she casts upon herself is lucid and severe.

> Que fais-je? (. . .)
> Mes crimes désormais ont comblé la mesure:
> Je respire à la fois l'inceste et l'imposture.
> Mes homicides mains, promptes à me venger,
> Dans le sang innocent brûlent de se plonger.
>
> IV, 6

In the same scene she resumes control of herself, and harshly drives away Œnone. Finally she freely decides to clear the memory of Hippolyte, and before taking poison, she makes a full and public confession to her husband who, even at this late stage, has not understood, or does not wish to understand. However formidable the pressures under which Phèdre is labouring, however criminal her silences, her final image is not one of

weakness and passive acquiescence. 'Neither guilty nor innocent,' Racine said; he might just as well have said both guilty
and innocent, for we cannot condemn her, nor can we fail to
condemn her.

But at this point there appears another unexpected element.
We may not condemn Phèdre, but *she* does. At the beginning
of the tragedy Phèdre has not betrayed her husband, or caused
the death of his son. Yet she wishes to end her life not just
because it is unbearable but because, she says,

> J'en ai trop prolongé la *coupable* durée.
>
> I, 3

Long before she has declared her love to Hippolyte, she feels a
criminal:

> J'ai conçu pour *mon crime* une juste terreur.
>
> I, 3

Although Phèdre has never yielded to her passion the mere
presence of passion in her seems to her a crime. Although
Venus is to her a real force, a divine power, she still condemns
herself for a love the origin of which is beyond her conscious
will. Not that the theme of revolt is absent in the play. To Venus
Phèdre speaks with a bitterness and a hatred which takes us
back to *La Thébaïde* and *Andromaque*. Like Jocaste in *La
Thébaïde* she could say:

> (. . .) un crime *involontaire*
> Devait-il attirer toute votre colère ?

Like Jocaste she could ironically exclaim:

> Voilà de ces grands Dieux la suprême justice !
> Jusques au bord du crime ils conduisent nos pas,
> Ils nous le font commettre et ne l'excusent pas.
>
> *Théb.* III, 2

Like Oreste she could say:

> Ta haine a pris plaisir à former ma misère.
>
> *Andr.* V, 5

Phèdre too accuses the Gods,

> (. . .) ces Dieux qui dans mon flanc
> Ont allumé le feu fatal à tout mon sang,
> Ces Dieux qui se sont fait une gloire cruelle
> De séduire le cœur d'une faible mortelle.
>
> *Ph.* II, 5

But Phèdre's condemnation is not just self-condemnation. The presence – a spiritual presence, like that of Venus – of Minos gives it an entirely new meaning, a religious or metaphysical significance. In Racine's tragedy Minos is more than the pallid figure of ancient mythology. He is the supreme Judge to whom all men will after their death answer for their deeds (an idea which is very weakly present in the old myths). He is also Phèdre's own father. His double character as Father and as Judge gives him a status he never had in Antiquity, and practically identifies him to the Christian God – or at least to a God who gives absolute, transcendent validity to those social or moral imperatives to which Phèdre has tried hard, if unsuccessfully, to conform herself. Social and moral values now have a supernatural source and a divine Guarantor. They are lifted above time and circumstance into a world of eternal, omnipresent essences. In the play this takes the form of a vision of an almost hallucinatory character, which is also a 'reconnaissance' by Phèdre of her true relationship to the world and to the Gods:

> Où me cacher? Fuyons dans la nuit infernale.
> Mais que dis-je? Mon père y tient l'urne fatale;
> Le Sort, dit-on, l'a mise en ses sévères mains:
> Minos juge aux enfers tous les pâles humains.
> Ah! combien frémira son ombre épouvantée,
> Lorsqu'il verra sa fille à ses yeux présentée,
> Contrainte d'avouer tant de forfaits divers,
> Et des crimes peut-être inconnus aux enfers!
> Que diras-tu, mon père, à ce spectacle horrible?
> Je crois voir de ta main tomber l'urne terrible,
> Je crois te voir, cherchant un supplice nouveau,
> Toi-même de ton sang devenir le bourreau.
>
> IV, 6

Phèdre's situation is therefore the most extreme form of the tragedy of the *impasse* from which, since *Mithridate* and *Iphigénie*, Racine seemed to be moving away. There is no way out for Phèdre: life is not only the tyranny of Venus; it also is an accusing ring of divine presences staring her out:

> Le ciel, tout l'univers est plein de mes aïeux.

But death offers no relief: it is no longer the ultimate shelter, the compassionate night of nothingness, but the promise of the Last Judgement and eternal torment. This, however, does not encompass the whole horror of the tragic universe Racine has created in *Phèdre*, for it is the universe of Venus and Neptune, as well as of Minos. It is a world in which the innocent are punished for crimes they have not committed, and a world in which an all-powerful divinity compels men and women to commit sins which an all-powerful divinity will punish for eternity. A world in which man passes from the incomprehensible injustice of the Gods of life to the no less incomprehensible 'justice' of the Gods of death. It is chaos in the mind of man, and anarchy among the Gods. It is a world which would be totally senseless and absurd, but for the fact that it seems infallibly to work against man. We are far from *Iphigénie*, far also from the haughty, defiant creator of Pyrrhus and Néron, far even from Greek tragedy: the heroic, clear-sighted vision of man's threatened, precarious condition in his great Hellenic models has turned in Racine to despair and melancholia.

The poetry of *Phèdre*

This is no doubt but a phase in Racine's tormented inner life, but it is an essential one. It is, at a certain moment of Racine's life, Racine's truth. And because it was his deepest, darkest truth, there is in *Phèdre* the highest, most splendid poetry he has created. The long years of resistance have exhausted Phèdre and, so to speak, eroded her power of resistance, her reason, and her will. Her endless vigil has all but finally stripped her of her vigilance, and in her 'trance-like reverie' (Lapp) it is indeed the rich substance of her dreams that is laid bare. If *Phèdre* is, as Racine strangely words it in his Preface, his most 'reasonable' production, it is perhaps in the extraordinary way – probably unique in his time – he has lucidly captured and fixed the fleeting messages from regions of the human psyche which were, in his time, far beyond the grasp of reason, and conveyed them through the consummate artistry of words, sounds, and rhythms, through the magic of imagery and music. Constantly, like the Rimbaldian 'voyant' in the 'déréglement de tous ses sens', Phèdre escapes from the narrow limits of the present or the actual, abolishing the immediate reality, evoking a wider, stranger one:

> Dieux! que ne suis-je assise à l'ombre des forêts!
> Quand pourrai-je, au travers d'une noble poussière,
> Suivre de l'œil un char fuyant dans la carrière!

> Noble et brillant auteur d'une triste famille, (. . .)
> Soleil, (. . .)

> Ariane, ma sœur, de quel amour blessée,
> Vous mourûtes aux bords où vous fûtes laissée!
>
> I, 3

Constantly the opposition of light and darkness assumes the force and the value of a symbol. From the blinding, accusing light of the Sun-God Phèdre retreats like a creature of the shadows:

> Vous vouliez vous montrer et revoir la lumière.
> Vous la voyez, Madame, et prête à vous cacher,
> Vous haïssez le jour que vous veniez chercher?
>
> I, 3

Hippolyte is the hero of light:

> Le jour n'est pas plus pur que le fond de (son) cœur.
>
> IV, 2

Even condemned by the Father Hippolyte and Aricie do not
fear the full light of the sun:

> Le ciel de leurs soupirs approuvait l'innocence (. . .)
> Tous les jours se levaient clairs et sereins pour eux.
> Et moi, triste rebut de la nature entière,
> Je me cachais au jour, je fuyais la lumière.
>
> IV, 6

Darkness is not only the darkness of shame, not only the darkness of death, it is 'la nuit infernale', the timeless darkness of
fear, guilt, and self-punishment, to which Phèdre finally con-
signs herself, cancelling herself from a world in which she feels
her mere presence is an outrage, which the very look of her eyes
is polluting, to which she can only give back the purity she
longed for by the total sacrifice of herself:

> Déjà je ne vois plus qu'à travers un nuage
> Et le ciel, et l'époux que ma présence outrage;
> Et la mort, à mex yeux dérobant la clarté,
> Rend au jour, qu'ils souillaient, toute sa pureté.
>
> V, 7

Phèdre is tragically alone at the moment of her death: no one,
not even her husband makes a gesture, utters a word of comfort or compassion. Yet she is not alone as Eriphile was, and
we do not doubt that Racine is with her, suffering with her, and,
perhaps, dying with her.

The Biblical Dramas

Racine's silence

Phèdre undoubtedly marked a climax in Racine's career, but it was the signal not of universal acclaim but of a concerted attack from his all too numerous enemies, who managed to have an obscure rival, Nicolas Pradon, hastily put together another *Phèdre*, which they noisily applauded. What fun they must have derived from such a neat little plot! They could hardly, however, have expected it would succeed so well: Racine appeared shattered; *Phèdre* was the last play he produced for the public, and for twelve years he wrote nothing for the stage.

This disproportion between the cause and the effect is such that ever since critics have pondered over Racine's silence. What he went through we can only try to reconstruct. What is certain is that, whereas the beginning of his creative career had been marked by a violent break with Port-Royal, he now became reconciled with his Jansenist masters. Within weeks his marriage had been arranged, as was the custom at the time, a marriage in which, one of his sons said admiringly, love or interest had no place. His wife had never read, and would never read, her husband's tragedies. All their children were brought up in the strictest Jansenist spirit; two of his daughters became nuns; to his son Louis – who derived it from Boileau – we owe most of the information and of the misinformation we possess on Racine's life; his eldest son, Jean-Baptiste, his father entreated never to show himself in a theatre. The traditional view was that Racine had seen the errors of his ways, realized that a playwright was *un empoisonneur public*, and chosen the good life.

Others, however, said that there was no need to suppose any crisis, that Racine was no longer a young man, and simply had nothing more to say (but he was thirty-seven!). Or that Racine had just received the highly honorable and very lucrative charge of Royal Historian: to him perhaps Louis le Grand appeared a more glamorous subject than some mythical Greek characters, and one that fully gratified his ambition. For it is true that Racine's retreat did not affect his social position: he spent much time at Court, and enjoyed the King's particular favour. But all such solutions imply that a work of art could be fabricated, or discontinued, in cold blood, which few serious psychologists will accept. Nor are we much inclined any more to delight in the sentimental picture of a Racine churchgoer and *père de famille* – the ageing, heavily bewigged courtier of his late portraits: Racine had a gift, an exceptional gift, and he smothered it. The reason does not come within the scope of such a study, but his silence looks more like a mutilation than an achievement.

Yet this silence was not after all to be final. Racine was to write two more plays, *Esther* (1689) and *Athalie* (1691), both directly derived from the Old Testament, both imbued with the spirit of Jansenism. Times had changed since Racine had first come to Court, twenty-five years before. The brilliant pageant that followed the young King and the *jeune Cour* everywhere had been replaced by the solemn, rigid etiquette of Versailles. The King was now fifty, and, partly under the influence of the austere Marquise de Maintenon, whom he had secretly married, the Court had taken the airs, if not the spirit, of devotion. The Marquise had founded at Saint-Cyr, near Versailles, a charitable institution for the education of girls of noble birth and poor means. As was the custom in seventeenth-century schools the pupils regularly performed in plays – even in some of Racine's tragedies, and they put so much conviction and passion in a performance of *Andromaque* that Madame de Maintenon asked Racine to provide her with more suitable material. Could he perhaps, 'in his spare time, write some kind of moral or historical poem, in which song would be mixed with music, and from which love would be entirely banished'? Racine could not deny a request from such an exalted origin.

Un ouvrage de piété

Esther was a great success, mainly perhaps because of the direct interest the King and the Marquise took in its production, so that it became a considerable event at Court, also because of its splendid costumes and décors. With the music of its choruses it reflected the increasing interest in the spectacular kind of theatre which had found its most brilliant expression in the operas of Lulli and Quinault. Racine's subject is taken from the *Book of Esther*. Aman, the evil minister, 'race d'Amalécite', hates the wise, virtuous Jew, Mardochée, who has not humbled himself before him. To revenge himself he has misled the King, Assuérus, into ordering the massacre of all the Jews in Persia. But he does not know that Esther is the niece and adopted daughter of Mardochée, who, thanks to his wisdom and foresight, has placed her on the throne and in the bed of the King. At the right moment Esther reveals her origin, and saves her people. The villainous Aman is hanged on the gallows he had prepared for Mardochée, who becomes the King's minister in his place.

It would be unfair to dwell too long on what Racine had first called *un ouvrage de piété tiré de l'Ecriture Sainte, propre à être récité et à être chanté*, and to treat it like one of his tragedies. It is not, however – how could it be? – quite unrelated to them. The situation is not unlike that of *Iphigénie*. Esther, in confessing her race, is also ready to die as a victim. But she remains a passive one, obedient to the voice of Mardochée, without love or passion to attach her to life, since all passion is of the flesh, and mere concupiscence, which would be a bad example to the *demoiselles de Saint-Cyr*. Hence her ashy, even dreary character. The King is at a much lower level of effectiveness than Agamemnon; Calchas, invisible but formidable in *Iphigénie*, in *Esther* occupies the centre of the stage: Mardochée, the man of God, the (adoptive) father of Esther, has displaced the temporal ruler: he is the true Father and the true King. In fact the moralistic intention is so bare as to be embarrassing: the wicked are wholly wicked, and sufficiently dehumanized for us to applaud their downfall without reservation; the good are good *ex officio*, and can be cruel with a good conscience. Assuérus, the Great King, is forgetful, extravagant, and childishly credulous; the bloodthirsty tyrant who has sanctioned the massacre of a whole race tenderly reassures his frightened spouse. Characters have neither depth nor substance or coherence. Whatever its extra-literary interest, psychological or biographical (for Racine certainly thought of the nuns of Port-Royal when he wrote the choruses of the *Jeunes Israélites*), even bearing in mind the circumstances, the young actresses who were to perform it, *Esther* cannot be said to be worthy of Racine.

The heathen Queen

Athalie, is drawn from the *Book of Kings*. Partly because the *dévots* had complained of the too worldly success of *Esther*, it was performed a couple of times only, privately, in front of the King and a few persons, without décors or costumes, which was a pity, as it particularly lends itself to spectacular staging: set in the very temple of Solomon, in the ninth century before Christ, it opens on one of the great Jewish Festivals,* and it ends with the solemn ceremony of the crowning of a King; it has been called the first great Romantic drama in France. As in *Esther*, but in a much more awesome way, the principal character is the Biblical God, but the narrow moralism of *Esther* is gone. Athalie is the daughter of Ahab and Jezebel, who are in the Bible the very incarnation of Evil. Queen of Judah, and a worshipper of Baal, she has seen her parents and her whole family exterminated at the call of the prophets, and she has, as a reprisal, massacred all the descendants of David – her own grandsons. Steeped in crime and impiety, Athalie is the enemy of God, she stands in the way of God's design, but there is in that barbaric, infernal figure something that goes far beyond the contemptible nastiness of Aman. Athalie is a great Queen, 'éclairée, intrépide', respected by her people and her neighbours. There is in her more than a little of imperial Agrippine. But her first appearance on the stage has the pathos of Phèdre: she is

* 'La Pentecôte', Racine says. That is to say the fiftieth day after Passover, the Feast of Weeks (Shavouth), not, as is often said, the Feast of Tabernacles, an Autumn festival.

staggering under the first of the powerful blows struck against
her by the invisible opponent who will, in the few hours of the
tragedy, destroy her:

> Non, je ne puis: tu vois mon trouble et ma faiblesse.
> Va, fais dire à Mathan qu'il vienne, qu'il se presse,
> Heureuse si je puis trouver par son secours
> Cette paix que je cherche et qui me fuit toujours.
>
> *Ath.* I, 3

Athalie is no abstract personification of Evil, in whose fall we
can find some kind of satisfaction or comfort. Athalie is a
human being, all too vulnerably human, whose resistance is
being sapped from within. Two terrifying dreams ('Me devrais-
je inquiéter d'un songe?') have left her shaken: the apparition
of her mother, Jezebel, an unforgettable one, gaudy and
sinister, like the made-up face of a corpse, has brought a
message of disaster:

> 'Le cruel Dieu des Juifs l'emporte aussi sur toi.
> 'Je te plains de tomber dans ses mains redoutables,
> 'Ma fille.' (. . .)
> Et moi, je lui tendais les mains pour l'embrasser.
> Mais je n'ai plus trouvé qu'un horrible mélange
> D'os et de chairs meurtris et traînés dans la fange,
> Que des chiens dévorants se disputaient entre eux.
>
> I, 5

A second dream has brought relief:

> Un jeune enfant couvert d'une robe éclatante, (. . .)
> J'admirais sa douceur, son air noble et modeste.

But the radiant apparition suddenly has turned against her, and
stabbed her. And then, as in the waking dreams of madness, the
nightmare has followed her in daylight. That very child, she
has just seen him, in the Jewish temple, with her own eyes. But
what was the heathen Queen doing in the Jewish temple?
Mathan, the High Priest of Baal no longer understands her:

> Grande Reine, est-ce ici votre place?
> Quel trouble vous agite, et quel effroi vous glace?
> Parmi vos ennemis que venez-vous chercher?
>
> I, 5

The Sacred Child

On the side of the Faithful there has been alarm and con-
sternation too. Facing the tragic figure of Athalie, the High
Priest of Iahweh, Joad is of an equally heroic stature. He it is
who, after his wife has rescued the infant left for dead, has
raised him secretly with his own children, Zacharie and Salo-
mith. For the true King of Israel, the lone survivor of the line of
David, to which God has promised a Messiah, the ancestor of
Christ is alive. Under a supposed name, ignorant of himself,
the child Eliacin has grown in the temple – just as the orphan
Racine had grown in Port-Royal – in the shadow of the formidable Father-figure to whom he owes his life, who dominates
the play as Mithridate or Agamemnon, or even Calchas or
Mardochée never did. For if Eliacin is the Sacred Child, who
embodies the stubborn hopes of the race, like Astyanax
miraculously preserved, on the other hand the Father, always
dangerous, always feared or disobeyed so far, is now at long
last accepted and trusted. A fundamental change in the very
structure of Racine's tragedy, and one of deep religious
significance.

. . . *cet esprit d'imprudence et d'erreur*

Athalie is rich with harmonics and resonances of this kind,
but it is also the most dramatic of Racine's plays. The unexpected encounter of Athalie and the child she does not know to be
Joas, her grandson, precipitates the action. Already Athalie's
advisers are suspicious. Who is this child?

> On le craint, tout est examiné.
>
> I, 5

Racine's Machiavellism finds its last exponent in Mathan,
another Acomat, who also happens to be a former rival of
Joad, and a renegade from the true cult. But to the violence and
cunning of his opponents Joad will oppose more effective
violence and cunning. Playing on the Queen's trust in Abner,
a limited but loyal soldier, on her greed for the supposed
treasures hidden in the temple, even on her attraction to the

child, he will finally draw her into the temple, whose massive gates will close upon her like jaws upon their prey:

> Grand Dieu, voici ton heure, on t'amène ta proie.
>
> V, 3

Joad will succeed because he knows how to play the ruthless game of Agrippine and Néron. But he will succeed above all because Athalie plays into his hands, and at the very beginning of the play his solemn invocation is a portent of what will happen:

> Daigne, daigne, mon Dieu, sur Mathan et sur elle
> Répandre cet esprit d'imprudence et d'erreur,
> De la chute des rois funeste avant-coureur.
>
> I, 2

Like Agrippine, Athalie will blindly stumble into the trap the High Priest has set for her, but the decisive factor in her final downfall will be the inexplicable interest the child Eliacin has awakened in her:

> Quel prodige nouveau me trouble et m'embarrasse?
> La douceur de sa voix, son enfance, sa grâce,
> Font insensiblement à mon inimitié
> Succéder . . . Je serais sensible à la pitié?
>
> II, 7

Athalie will finally perish not through her crimes but through her love: we are far indeed from the simplifications of *Esther*. To the enchanting Eliacin she offers riches, pleasures, a throne:

> Vous voyez, je suis reine, et n'ai point d'héritier. (. . .)
> Je prétends vous traiter comme mon propre fils.
>
> II, 7

In the blandishments of the Queen there are echoes of the possessive mothers of Racine, from Agrippine to Phèdre, and of the jealous *amantes* who, like Hermione and Roxane, demanded love by right or by force. In Athalie they are all finally rejected. For if Joas has behind him a long line of Hebrew Kings, he also has as his literary ancestors all those Racinian heroes who rebelled against the domineering women who offered the choice between love or death, and Athalie is the most ambivalent of them all. In fact, in that dramatic scene in which Athalie has silenced Josabet, the decision is in the hands of the frail child facing the Queen alone. And if the Child rejects the Mother, it is not in favour of another more tender, more appealing love (by putting a child in the centre of his drama Racine has successfully excluded Eros from his tragedy); it is for the Father, the man of God, the very image of God on earth:

> Quel père
> Je quitterais! Et pour . . .
> – Hé bien?
> – Pour quelle mère!
>
> II, 7

Joad's vision

Yet what gives the tragedy its full meaning is Joad's great prophetic vision placed almost exactly in the centre of the play, immediately preceding Joas' crowning, and Athalie's final assault. There is no dramatic necessity for it, and it could be excised from the *action* without difficulty, but it is an essential part of the religious, cosmic, tragic aspect of the play, and it must colour our impression of everything that follows. It is a three-fold vision, the meaning of which remains obscure to the assistants and to Joad himself, but just as Athalie's fearful dreams seem to pull her back into the past, and into death and the *nuit infernale*, Joad's visions open distant vistas into the future. The first one is of a High Priest lying murdered in the temple: Joad does not know that he is looking at his own son, Zacharie, who will succeed him in his high office, and that the murderer will be Joas, the graceful child who owes him his life and his crown. The second one shows the lamentable crowd of the Jews herded like cattle into the captivity of Babylon, their king murdered, Solomon's temple ablaze. The last one is of the age-old Jewish dream of a new Jerusalem, to which all Kings will pay homage, the Jerusalem that is not of this world. Thus the triumphant ending of *Athalie* falls back into perspective;

it is but a moment in eternity. The dawn of hope that is the
return of the true King and the downfall of the usurper is but a
false dawn. Joad will have laboured and conquered in vain. The
final curse of Athalie, vanquished but defiant to the end, will be
fulfilled:

> Voici ce qu'en mourant lui souhaite sa mère.
> Que dis-je, souhaiter? je me flatte, j'espère
> Qu'indocile à ton joug, fatigué de ta loi,
> Fidèle au sang d'Achab, qu'il a reçu de moi,
> Conforme à son aïeul, à son père semblable,
> On verra de David l'héritier détestable
> Abolir tes honneurs, profaner ton autel,
> Et venger Athalie, Achab et Jézabel.

V, 6

Athalie is dragged out of the temple, and killed, leaving Joas
terrified: the new reign has begun – with a matricide.

What then is the difference between the world of *Britannicus*
and *Phèdre* and that of *Athalie*? Men and women are again
assailed by irresistible passions: Athalie can no more resist the
love that stays her hand and saves Joas than Phèdre can resist
Venus. Incomprehensible Powers, like Vigny's Destinies, hold
mankind in their claws. The God of *Athalie* is as cruel and as
pitiless as the God of *Phèdre*: he is the 'cruel Dieu des Juifs',
the 'impitoyable Dieu (qui) seul (a) tout conduit'. He is as
baffling as Fate in *La Thébaïde*: his ways are not our ways:

> Le Seigneur a daigné parler.
> Mais ce qu'à son prophète il vient de révéler,
> Qui pourra nous le faire entendre?
> S'arme-t-il pour nous défendre?
> S'arme-t-il pour nous accabler?
>
> O promesse! ô menace! ô ténébreux mystère!
> Que de maux, que de biens sont prédits tour a tour!
> Comment peut-on avec tant de colère
> Accorder tant d'amour?

III, 7

The God of *Athalie* is, like the God of Jansenius, a 'hidden
God', an absent God. There is no way of forcing his inter-

vention by prayer or by good deed, for fallen men are incapable of any true good deed; men deserve nothing:

> Ils ne s'assurent point sur leurs propres mérites.
>
> III, 7

Murder and deceit have been Athalie's weapons; they are also those of Joad, for there are no others in the fallen world. No man is 'good' or 'bad', for all are sinners. God himself, working in a world that is utterly corrupt, makes use of corrupt men for his own design.

The difference is of course in Racine's belief that there is such a design. It is in Racine's attitude of acceptance and hope; a hope that is dim and remote, the hope of a redemption that seems to be indefinitely postponed, a hope that nothing seems to substantiate in the world such as Racine sees it. Like Pascal's *pari*, it is an act of faith, as irrational as the act of refusal and rebellion of the young Racine. It is indeed remarkable that a theatre that was so often seen as a 'courtly theatre', with a field of experience limited to a narrow range of passions in a narrow social stratum, should include the two major responses man can give to the enigma of his life.

NOTE

On Reading Racine

With few exceptions (the stanzas and the oracle in *La Thébaïde*, the letter in *Bajazet*, the choruses in *Esther* and *Athalie*), Racine's verse is the *alexandrin*. *Alexandrins* often appear to students as either Classical or Romantic. The Romantics, it is said, shifted the caesura, practised the *enjambement*, gave the *alexandrin* a new flexibility and variety. It is only too easy to infer from this that the Classical *alexandrin* had none of these qualities: with its regular caesura at the sixth, and its compulsory stop at the twelfth syllable, it treads with heavy, equal steps, mechanical and stiff, a torment for the ear and for the mind. And this is indeed what it too often sounds like in classrooms:

> Oui puisQUE je reTROUve / un AMI si fiDEle /
> Ma forTUne va PRENdre / une FACE nouVELle /
> Et déJA son courROUX / semble s'Etre adouCI /
> Depuis QU'ELle a pris SOIN / de nous REjoindre ICI. /

Rhythm of course does depend on the regular return of stresses, but stress in French is – normally – on the last syllable, not of each word, but of each group of words. This simple rule changes the lines spoken by Oreste at the beginning of *Andromaque* into something different:

> OUI, puisque je reTROUve un AMI si fiDEle,
> Ma forTUne va PRENdre une FACE nouVELle;
> Et déJA son courROUX SEMble s'être adouCI,
> DePUIS qu'elle a pris SOIN de nous reJOINdre ICI.

If for a moment we consider the *hémistiche* alone, the only rule is that its last syllable cannot be unstressed: the other stress, or stresses, may be anywhere, or nowhere. It is true that examples of *alexandrins* in which the stresses are on the 2nd and 6th, or 3rd and 6th, or 4th and 6th are more frequent than others:

2 and 6: DEPUIS qu'elle a pris SOIN   SURTOUT je redouTAIS
3 and 6: un AMI si fiDEle   une FACE nouVELle
4 and 6: de nous reJOINdre ICI   Vous me tromPIEZ, SeiGNEUR.

but any other combination is possible:

1 and 6: OUI, puisque je reTROUve   SEMble s'être adouCI
1, 3, 6:   QUOI? votre Ame à l'aMOUR
2, 4, 6:   ALlez. Et NOUS, MaDAme

or only one stress on the last syllable, as in the second *hémistiche* of these two lines:

   Et que vous MONtrent-ILS qui ne vous averTISSE
   Qu'il FAUT qu'on me resPEcte et que l'on m'obéISSE?

If we now remember that the twelfth-syllable *alexandrin* is the real unit, not the *hémistiche*, we can see that each variety of *hémistiche* can combine with itself and with all the others to produce a large number of variations.

The first eight lines of Oreste's speech to Pyrrhus (*Andr.* I, 2), offer eight different forms of *alexandrins*:

Avant que tous les Grecs vous parlent par ma voix,	2	6		8	12
Souffrez que j'ose ici me flatter de leur choix,	2 4 6			9	12
Et qu'à vos yeux, Seigneur, je montre quelque joie	4	6		8	12
De voir le fils d'Achille et le vainqueur de Troie.	2 4 6			10	12
Oui, comme ses exploits nous admirons vos coups:	1	6		10	12
Hector tomba sous lui, Troie expira sous vous;	2 4 6 7			10	12
Et vous avez montré, par une heureuse audace,		6		10	12
Que le fils seul d'Achille a pu remplir sa place.	3 4 6			10	12

This is a public speech addressed to the King by an ambassador, and the unusual number of stresses slows it down, and emphasizes its official, deliberate character.

As for the sixth-syllable caesura, it may sometimes be strongly marked (e.g., in an antithesis):

> Hector tomba sous lui, // Troie expira sous vous.

But in Racine it is usually more discreet, and in some cases hardly audible. What is more remarkable is that there may be other *coupes*, or stops, which may be more important than the caesura:

> Oui, / puisque je retrouve un ami si fidèle,

A strong stop after the first, second, or third syllable gives strong emphasis to the word it isolates, and in so far as it breaks the usual rhythm it may express a sudden movement of passion:

> Moi! // Voilà les soupçons / dont vous êtes capable! /

> Poursuis. // Tu n'as pas fait ce pas pour reculer. /
> > *Brit*. V, 6

> S'il voulait . . . // Mais l'ingrat ne veut que m'outrager. /
> > *Andr*. II, 1

> Non, je ne puis: // tu vois mon trouble et ma faiblesse.
> > *Ath*. I, 3

Dialogue, especially animated dialogue, in which lines are divided between characters, introduces more variety. Numerous stops may suggest agitation, emphasize accumulation:

> A combien de chagrins / il faut que je m'apprête: /
> Que d'importunités! /
> > – Quoi donc? / Qui vous arrête,
> Seigneur? /
> > – Tout: // Octavie, / Agrippine, / Burrhus, /
> Sénèque, / Rome entière, / et trois ans de vertus. /
> > *Brit*. II, 2

> Où suis-je? / Qu'ai-je fait? / Que dois-je faire encore? /
> > *Andr*. V, 1

Pourquoi l'assassiner? / Qu'a-t-il fait? / A quel titre? /
Qui te l'a dit? /

Andr. V, 3

Combined with numerous stresses they give the line the quality
of a whiplash:

Vous, / dont j'ai pu laisser vieillir l'ambition
Dans les honneurs obscurs de quelque légion,
Et moi, / qui sur le trône ai suivi mes ancêtres,
Moi, / fille, / femme, / sœur, / et mère de vos maîtres.

Brit. I, 2

And there is of course the question of *enjambement*. It has
been said sometimes that there is *enjambement* when the meaning of a line is not complete without the following line. This is a
misleading definition, as it seems to imply that there is *enjambement* whenever the sentence is not completed in one line, and
that Racine or Corneille would usually express themselves in
sentences of one line, which is of course not the case. In this
long sentence of eight lines it cannot be said that there is any
real *enjambement*:

Malgré tout mon amour, si dans cette journée,
Il ne m'attache à lui par un juste hyménée;
S'il ose m'alléguer une odieuse loi;
Quand je fais tout pour lui, s'il ne fait tout pour moi;
Dès le même moment, sans songer si je l'aime,
Sans consulter enfin si je me perds moi-même,
J'abandonne l'ingrat, et le laisse rentrer
Dans l'état malheureux d'où j'ai su le tirer.

Baj. I, 3

But it is possible to speak of *enjambement* when the beginning
of a line can be said to belong *more* to the previous line than to
the following one. The interpellations, 'Seigneur', 'Madame',
'Prince', or the name of a character are often used in that way,
and the punctuation makes it quite clear:

Vous me donnez des noms qui doivent me surprendre,
Madame: / on ne m'a pas instruite à les entendre.

Iph. II, 5

Je ne vous flatte point, je me plaignais de vous,
Burrhus: / je vous ai crus tous deux d'intelligence.

Brit. IV, 3

> Cet honneur vous regarde, et j'ai fait choix de vous,
> Pharnace. / Allez, soyez ce bienheureux époux.
>
> *Mithr*. III, 1

Such weak *enjambements* often have little value except to give the rhythm more flexibility, but they can also broaden it, and lengthen the line with considerable effect, at the same time giving strong emotional emphasis to the word thus underlined:

> 'Je te plains de tomber dans ses mains redoutables,
> 'Ma fille,' // En achevant ces mots épouvantables, (. . .)
>
> *Ath*. I, 5

> Quoi! Céphise, / j'irai voir expirer encor
> Ce fils, / ma seule joie, et l'image d'Hector?
>
> *Andr*. III, 8

One famous example has exceptional energy:

> Prenez garde, Seigneur: vos invincibles mains
> Ont de monstres sans nombre affranchi les humains;
> Mais tout n'est pas détruit, et vous en laissez vivre
> Un . . . // Votre fils, Seigneur, me défend de poursuivre.
>
> *Ph*. V, 2

All the previous remarks must be read with the understanding that, within the framework of the twelve-syllable line and an accent (of variable force) on the sixth and twelfth syllable, much is left to the reader's feeling, or the actor's interpretation, touching the intonation, the speed and tempo not only of a passage but of a single line, and even the stressing. For stressing has in French a great flexibility, and emotion results not as in English in reinforcing the stress (NEver!) but in shifting it (JAmais!). Rather than by stops and stresses Racine's verse might be better represented by a sinuous line, now rapid, now slow, now rising, now falling, now continuous and sustained, and to describe it, the vocabulary of music comes naturally to mind; there are notes of long or short duration; there is *crescendo* and *decrescendo*, *accelerando*, *staccato*, *sostenuto*, *largo*, *agitato* . . .

In fact, apart from rhythm and intonation, *enjambements*, stresses and stops, the poet, like the musician, also has at his disposal the suggestive power of sounds. Sounds are what gives his verse its full emotional and sensuous impact. It would be futile to attempt to give each letter a distinct function or emotional mood. But they have a resonance and a pitch that is their own. Open, loud vowels as in: 'âme', 'air', 'heure', 'or', have a much more sonorous quality than close, soft ones, as in: 'doux', 'lune', or the so-called 'e muet'. 'Vie' has a higher pitch than 'feu' or 'beau'. A triumphant line like:

> SouverAIne des MERS qui vous DOIvent PORTer
>
> *Mithr.* I, 3

owes much of its suggestive effect to its broad, long vowels, nearly all placed in stressed syllables. Whereas the anguished call of Phèdre to her dead sister ends in a sorrowful, flute-like murmur:

> Ariane, ma SOEUR, de quel amOUR blessée,
> VOUS MOURUTES aux bords OU VOUS FUTES laissée.
>
> *Ph.* I, 3

with the internal echoes of the OU's and U's. Very different is the effect produced by the *staccato* of short, dry vowels, in the hasty, furtive dialogue of Andromaque with her confidant:

> Il a promis mon fils.
>   – Il ne l'a pas donné.
>
> *Andr.* III, 6

Phèdre's unbearable torment is in the insistent repetition of I's:

> Tout m'afflIge at me nuIt et conspIre à me nuIre.
>
> *Ph.* I, 3

Hermione's longing and grief and despair is conveyed not only by words but by the long, vibrant, muffled nasal sounds, reinforced by the alliteration of M's:

> Je t'aimais inconstant; qu'aurais-je fait fidèle?
> Et même en ce moment où ta bouche cruelle
> Vient si tranquillement m'annoncer le trépas, . . .
>
> *Andr.* IV, 5

S and CH, F and V can be long-drawn if necessary:

> Pourquoi me forcez-vous vous-même à vous haïr?
>
> *Andr*. III, 7

whereas instantaneous explosives like P, T, K, B, D, G, as well
as the hard French R, have a harsher quality, or a higher charge
of energy, than M, N, or L.

> . . . il faut ou périr ou régner.
>
> *Andr*. III, 7

Explosives combined with R's and S's, and the hammering
effect of the 'rime surabondante' (rare in Racine) convey the
full threat of Pyrrhus' anger and desire:

> Mon cœur, désespéré d'un an d'ingratitude,
> Ne peut plus de son sort souffrir l'incertitude.
>
> *Andr*. III, 7

These are only a few of the remarks that could be made about
Racine's verse, and their only purpose is to emphasize how
important it is to *listen* to his poetry.

Select Bibliography

COLLECTED WORKS

Œuvres, éd. P. Mesnard (Les Grands Ecrivains de France), 8 vol. 1865–73.

Œuvres complètes, éd. R. Picard, Pléiade, Gallimard, 1950. 2 vol. Theatre in vol. I.

Œuvres complètes, éd. Clarac, L'Intégrale, Seuil and Macmillan, New York, 1962.

SINGLE PLAYS

Numerous French school editions: Classiques Larousse, Classiques du peuple (Andromaque and Britannicus), Bordas, etc. Also see J. Dubu, Lettres d'Uzès, Uzès, Péladan, 1963.

French texts with English notes and introduction:

Britannicus, ed. P. Butler, Cambridge University Press, 1967.

Bérénice, ed. Maguinness, Manchester University Press, 1956.

Phèdre, ed. Roy C. Knight, Manchester University Press, 1955.

Athalie, ed. P. France, Oxford University Press, 1966.

TRANSLATIONS

J. Cairncross, Andromache and other plays (Britannicus and Berenice), Penguin Classics, 1967.

— Phaedra and other plays (Iphigeneia, Athaliah) Penguin Classics, 1963.

Roy C. Knight, Phaedra, Edinburgh Bilingual Library (2), Edinburgh University Press, 1971.

GENERAL

H. C. Lancaster, A History of French Dramatic Literature in the 17th century, Johns Hopkins Press and Presses Universitaires Françaises, 1929–42. Racine: Pts IV and V.

A. Adam, Histoire de la Littérature française au XVIIe siècle. Domat, 1948–56. Racine: vol. IV.

BIOGRAPHY

R. Picard, *La carrière de J. Racine*, Gallimard, 1956.

G. Brereton, *J. Racine. A critical biography*, London, Cassell, 1951.

CRITICISM

R. Barthes, *Sur Racine*, Ed. du Seuil, 1963.

P. Bénichou, *Morales du grand siècle*, Gallimard, 1948 (Chapters on Racine and Jansenism). Transl. by E. Hughes: *Man and ethics: studies on French classicism*, New York, Anchor Books, 1971.

P. Butler, *Classicisme et baroque dans l'oeuvre de Racine*, Nizet, 1959. Repr. 1971.

L. Goldmann, *Le dieu caché. Etude sur la vision tragique dans les 'Pensées' de Pascal et dans le théâtre de Racine*, Gallimard, 1955.

— Translated by Philip Thody, *The hidden God*, Routledge and Kegan Paul and Humanities Press.

J. D. Hubert, *Essais d'exégèse racinienne. Les secrets témoins*, Nizet, 1956.

R. C. Knight, *Racine et la Grèce*, Boivin, 1950.

— *Racine. Modern Judgements. Selection of critical essays*, Macmillan, 1969.

J. C. Lapp, *Aspects of Racinian tragedy*, University of Toronto Press, 1955.

C. Mauron, *L'Inconscient dans l'œuvre et la vie de Racine*, Corti, 1969.

G. May, *Tragédie cornélienne, tragédie racinienne. Etude sur les sources de l'intérêt dramatique*, Urbana, University of Illinois Press, 1948.

G. Pocock, *Corneille and Racine. Problems of tragic form*, Cambridge University Press, 1973.

M. Turnell, *J. Racine dramatist*, London, Hamilton, 1972.

E. Vinaver, *Racine et la poésie tragique*, Nizet, 1951 (Rev. ed. 1963).

— Translated by P. M. Jones, *Racine and poetic tragedy*, Manchester University Press, 1955.

— *Racine. Principes de la tragédie en marge de la Poétique d'Aristote*, Manchester University Press, 1944.

BIBLIOGRAPHY

D. C. Cabeen and J. Brody, *A critical bibliography of French Literature*, vol. III: *The seventeenth century*, Syracuse University Press, 1961.

The Year's work in Modern Language Studies.